The Business of Music Management

The Business of Music Management

How to Survive and Thrive in Today's Music Industry

Tom Stein

BUSINESS EXPERT PRESS

Leader in applied, concise business books

The Business of Music Management: How to Survive and Thrive in Today's Music Industry

Copyright © Business Expert Press, LLC, 2021.

Cover design by Charlene Kronstedt

Interior design by Exeter Premedia Services Private Ltd., Chennai, India

First published in 2021 by
Business Expert Press, LLC
222 East 46th Street, New York, NY 10017
www.businessexpertpress.com

ISBN-13: 978-1-95334-966-8 (paperback)
ISBN-13: 978-1-95334-967-5 (e-book)

Business Expert Press Sports and Entertainment Management and
Marketing Collection

Collection ISSN: 2333-8644 (print)
Collection ISSN: 2333-8652 (electronic)

First edition: 2021

10 9 8 7 6 5 4 3 2 1

Testimonials

"By far the best current guide to help you succeed in the music industry in 2021+. Great overview, especially the specific action steps at the end of each section. If you're ambitious, read this and act on it now!" —**Derek Sivers, Founder, CD Baby**

"Easy to digest book on how to make a living and find success in the music industry today." —**Lauren Gehle, Berklee College of Music Student**

"Tom Stein is a real shaman when it comes to the business of music. His knowledge is vast. He writes fluently and clearly, he is thorough yet organized, and you can't stop reading him. Most importantly, the information he lays out for the reader of his book is overwhelmingly useful and essential for every musician—from the wannabe to the professional and experienced—who wants to succeed or simply do better business. Recommended—you need this book!" —**Ady Cohen, Film Composer, Professor, Speaker (Israel)**

"An incredible piece of work that blends a number of different disciplines including business, communication, psychology, leadership, interpersonal communication, sales, marketing, and more that all point toward the music industry and succeeding in it. Bravo." —**Bobby Borg, Author of *Business Basics for Musicians* and *Music Marketing for the DIY Musician***

"Tom's book provides essential, practical and real-world strategies and advice that melds art with business that not only informs, but also inspires a level of confidence for readers to successfully manage their own artistic journey and career." —**Sean P. Hagon, Associate Dean of Career Education and Services, Berklee College of Music**

"Tom Stein is a master of music business and planning. He is a leading figure in management, career planning, and the general business industry. Mr. Stein enlightens his students and colleagues in every aspect. This book is a *masterpiece of his years of experience. It's a brilliant must-have book for every musician. I strongly recommend this book to my colleagues."* —**Utar Artun, Award winning composer, arranger, pianist, percussionist, and educator (Turkey/USA)**

"Tom Stein shows a deep and profound understanding of the music business and music industry. Through his personal teaching experience and years of research in a field of music business, communication, psychology, leadership in this book he covers everything that young musicians should know before entering the world of music." —**Gojko Damjanic, Educational Consultant GDEduConsulting (USA)**

"Tom Stein operates from a base of exhaustive specific knowledge and direct experience more than most people I know. This deeply generous book not only draws from seemingly every conceivable force connected to the business of music business, but mentors you through some "soul searching" as you build your own pathways to successfully navigate this maze." —**Samuel D. Skau, Senior Consultant for Strategy and Project Management, Gaudium Artopia, Center for the Performing and Visual Arts, Hyderabad (India)**

"Growing up, we all have dreams. To be an astronaut, a firefighter, or a rockstar. We just don't necessarily know how to make our dreams a reality. Tom's book provides the blueprint for how to bring the rockstar dream into fruition." —**Jonny Havey, CPA, MBA | Co-Founder VP Legacies**

Description

The book's focus is on successful music entrepreneurship and career development in the global music and entertainment industry.

Who Is It For?

High school and college students, including graduate level, who are embarking on careers in the global music industry. Students from abroad seeking to study in the United States or in other Anglophile countries, individuals preparing to enter the global entertainment industry, and adults interested in pursuing full- or part-time careers in music, or already working in related fields, such as event management, sports, experiential communications, or broadcasting, will also benefit. Besides students and careerists, the book is useful for university and college faculty, administrators, or course developers seeking to establish music industry educational programs because it highlights specific areas for curricular content and development.

What Is It About?

The list of specialized occupations filled by musicians is lengthy, for example, performer, producer, arranger, composer, songwriter, lyricist, music editor, publicist, recording engineer, conductor, sound technician, manager, entertainment lawyer, promoter, booking agent, tour manager, music educator, vocal coach, private instructor, music supervisor, music programmer, electronic DJ. There are also careers ancillary to music, such as event organizer, music therapist, radio station director, art director, advertising director, or entertainment director.

Music as an industry is multifaceted and is a subset of the broader entertainment industry which includes sports, cinema, broadcasting, and creative digital media. Music plays an important role in advertising, marketing, video games, film, and digital media, and there are tie-ins to tourism, restaurant, fashion, and the hospitality industries. The entertainment and creative industries in aggregate are viewed as a potential growth area by governments and by commercial concerns and often targeted and supported as a tool for sustainable international trade, plus economic, social, and cultural development. There is even such a thing as music diplomacy, as a component of cultural or "soft power" diplomacy.

As with many professions, the set of skills, knowledge, and strategies required to become successfully employed in music and its related fields are not the same set of skills needed to do the actual jobs. Young musicians and others with the ambition to work in the music industry are often baffled by the many options available, conflicting information, and the lack of a clear path to success. They are thirsty for balanced and reliable knowledge and clear direction on how to prepare for a career in the industry. Universities, colleges, and specialty training schools offer programs designed to help individuals prepare for careers in music, leading to certificates, diplomas, or degrees, including at the graduate level. But the focus of the trainings and curricula are often only on the skills needed to perform the work and not on how to access the work through careful career preparation and entrepreneurial thinking. There is a dearth of relevant information about how to access the opportunities, leverage the training and the networks gained in school, and how to succeed through meeting the true demands of the industry. This book aims to fill this need.

Many of the most successful people working in the field have benefited from formal training, while others did not have access to specialized programs or chose to study in another field perhaps deemed more "practical," for example, music education, finance, technology, science, or business. It is crucial that aspiring music professionals learn all they can about the specialized business of music and how to prepare for entry to the field, as many musicians ultimately become self-employed as independent business people, or will work in a business.

What Will the Reader Gain?

The reader of the book will gain vital and accurate knowledge about how the music business works, how musicians get paid for their work, and the legal framework for conducting business in the music industry. They will learn to effectively recognize, create, and plan for leveraging real opportunities and learn useful techniques for overcoming the inevitable obstacles to success in a rapidly changing industry sector. Readers will gain valuable insights into the niche they might fill with their own career and learn techniques to help them discover their unique path to success. The reader will come away with a much better understanding of the scope and demands of this dynamic industry sector.

Attitudes that contribute to success in the global music and entertainment industries will be presented, examined, and contextualized through illuminating case studies along with judicious storytelling. Topics will include how to start and lead a music-related business (entrepreneurship and executive leadership), business plan writing, social entrepreneurship, branding and marketing music (including viral social media marketing), technology, finance, revenue streams in the industry, and career planning. The reader will come away better prepared to enter and to compete in the global music industry with a slew of concrete strategies for success in creating, marketing, and monetizing musical content.

Keywords

music; music business; music industry; music management; music careers; music entrepreneurship; music marketing; entertainment; entertainment business; entertainment marketing; music education; artist entrepreneur; music artist; music production; songwriting; entertainment industry; video game music; music composition; film music; film scoring; scoring for visual media; music teacher; music streaming; music concerts

Contents

Preface

If you are reading this book it is because you have an interest in how the music industry works. You might be grappling with the prospect of choosing or defining your future music career and have questions about how to find your niche in the music field. The main purpose of this book is to demystify many of the crucial parts of the music industry, so that you can formulate some specific goals for your career, learn to identify opportunities, recognize obstacles to success, adopt strategies to get around the obstacles, and think rationally and clearly about where you fit in both today's and the future music industry.

Having worked in the music industry for decades as a performer, manager, agent, promoter, producer, tour director, conductor, arranger, contractor, consultant, and a professor, I've formed well-developed ideas about techniques and strategies that work. Over several decades of teaching music industry courses to bright and talented college students, I've witnessed first-hand the challenges and successes of my current and former students who've applied the techniques presented in this book. Importantly, I discovered how these techniques and strategies can be effectively taught and learned by anyone seeking a career in music.

There are many excellent books available about the music business, and about business in general. In writing this book I wanted to accomplish three things to set the book apart from all the others. First, while the book is about the music industry, I draw from other areas of business integrally, to help the reader better understand the business of music in the context of other business sectors. As a subsector of entertainment, media, advertising, and other fields, music integrates with numerous outside business sectors and subsectors, and I wanted readers to get a sense of where music fits in a much larger scheme and order of things and to learn how to strategically draw from best practices in other related and unrelated industries.

Second, I will provide a philosophy of leadership, service, and artistry that is directly connected to self-actualization through music as a business career. This philosophy leads to a greater understanding of music business management and will show how music careers can be accelerated with knowledge and application of executive leadership skills, business planning, marketing psychology, branding strategies, social entrepreneurship, organizational behavior, and other entrepreneurial and organizational approaches. We will address ways to adjust your own thinking to enhance your prospects for success. This will include the cultivation of specific meta-skills and recommended action steps to support your continued success.

These mental attitudes and skills are not exclusive to the music business. Fledgling entrepreneurs must look beyond their own industry for know-how, approaches, and inspiration. The modern contributions of Steve Jobs, Bill Gates, Jack Ma, Richard Branson, Elon Musk, Mark Cuban, Warren Buffet, and other business leaders who've become household names are well documented and have inspired the recent generation of would-be entrepreneurs, as have business icons from previous generations.

Though they came from different industries, Andrew Carnegie, Thomas Edison, Henry Ford, Harvey Firestone, Conrad Hilton, Ray Croc, Lee Iacocca, and Jack Welch all had one thing in common besides success: their thinking. They worked smart as well as hard. There's been plenty of research into how these iconic business leaders thought about their work, their attitudes about business and life, how they dealt with inevitable failures, and the psychology which enabled their enduring success. The study of executive leadership and the attendant psychology of success has not yet crossed over into the music business literature, until now.

Finally, the reader will be guided through step-by-step processes and shown methodologies to help to express a music idea as a complete business plan. In this way, the avid reader can integrate their newly gained knowledge of the business of music management into their own personal musical journey. The creation of the plan should prepare you, the reader, to confidently take the next steps in pursuit of your music and life goals.

This book will take you on an important journey of guided learning, as you read about and assimilate not only the crucial business knowledge, strategies, and information, but the self-knowledge, attitudes, and thinking that will enable you to achieve lasting success with your music. You will gain the satisfaction and peace of mind that come from knowing you are becoming the best possible version of yourself. You will learn what it takes to truly succeed in today's competitive and demanding music industry.

For the musician and artist starting a career in the music industry, the path from idea to reality is not as complicated as it might seem. That doesn't mean it's easy: It's not. Besides a little luck, the strategies, knowledge, encouragement, and inspiration you find in this book will serve as useful and welcome companions on your own path to success as a musician and artist. In summary, you are holding in your hands a book that fuses your musical ambitions with the business reality and will instruct you in the next concrete steps you can and should take to move confidently in the direction of your dreams.

Tom Stein
2021

Acknowledgments

Writing a book on the music industry is not a solo endeavor, and there are many people who contributed in meaningful ways to turning my goal of writing this book into reality.

My publisher, Business Expert Press, the editors, and my "thought partner" Deborah Ager from Radiant Media Labs worked at the early and later stages to help this book take form, to order the content, and to make it presentable. They kept me on point and held me accountable to the vision I wanted to present. Thanks to Eddy Skau for creating all the images.

My colleagues at Berklee College of Music in the Professional Music Department all contributed important knowledge and ideas at opportune times over many years: Department Chairs, Deans, and Professors Sean Hagon, Kenn Brass, Chee-Ping Ho, Jes Sarin-Perry, Joe Bennett, Bob Mulvey, Cristy Catt, Linda Gorham, Kirstie Wheeler, Jimena Bermejo, and Erin Raber.

I'm grateful to so many other special musicians and talented music business people I've learned from over the years, not only for their business acumen, but for their musical talent which has been so inspiring, and continues to be: Rob Rose, Donna McElroy, Ken Zambello, Richard Evans, Sal DiFusco, Kevin Harris, Steve Heck, Casey Scheuerell, Wolf Ginandes, Sam Skau, Gojko Damjanic, Fil Ramil, Tino Sanchez, Utar Artun, Dennis Cecere, George Garzone, Hal Crook, Bobby Stanton, Ed Tomassi, John LaPorta, Phil Wilson, Cory Harding, Brian Walkely, Bob Gay, Bob Talalla, Jackie Beard, Jeff Stout, Dino Govoni, Bora Uslusoy, Larry Watson, and many more. To be a part of such a vibrant community of creative musicians has been one of the greatest blessings of my life.

I'm grateful to and indebted to my many outstanding students who have kept me curious and in many cases taught me more than I taught them. To see them achieve new heights day after day and year after year is the greatest reward I've received from my career as a professor.

I'd also like to thank my good friend Rick Petralia, one of the best sales professionals I've ever met.

And of course I am super grateful for the enduring support of my lovely wife Burcu and musical daughter Sara Sandra.

Introduction

I was a small-town boy growing up with big-time dreams. Born at the close of the 1950s, my earliest memories are from the turbulent 1960s: the Kennedy and Martin Luther King assassinations, the Vietnam War, the Hippies and then the Yippies, the Black Panthers, and the Moon Landing. These historical events are embedded in my memory, but even more, the music of this time and shortly after is embedded in my psyche. It seems like the AM radio was always on (this was before cassettes, 8-tracks, or CDs) and the popular music of the day was mesmerizing. Our heroes were The Beatles, Eric Clapton, Jimi Hendrix, The Monkees, The Doors, The Who, The Kinks, The Rolling Stones, Richie Havens, Roy Orbison, Bob Dylan, Burt Bacharach, Aretha Franklin, Janis Joplin, Trini Lopez, Sonny and Cher, Sly and the Family Stone, Jethro Tull, Yes, the Grateful Dead, Led Zeppelin, Deep Purple, Nielson, Joni Mitchell, Sly and the Family Stone, Santana, Johnny and Edgar Winter—we were surrounded by this incredible music all the time. What strikes me now as interesting is that we liked the same music as our parents. My house was filled with LP-33rpm records in the heyday of vinyl albums. As the 1960s turned into the 1970s, rock music was flowering and the airwaves were enchanting to a young boy attracted to the music.

I also had access to a piano and a guitar. By the time I was 10 years old I could play Beatles and Bob Dylan songs, as well as some television theme songs from popular shows. As a young teenager I set myself to becoming proficient on the guitar. By the time I was 16 I knew that music would be my career choice. However, my parents were not in agreement with this. I was told that music was only a hobby, and I should choose a career that would provide me with a stable and secure living, like being an architect, a doctor, or a lawyer. My mother even suggested I choose a trade such as plumbing. ANYTHING but music. Musicians were poor, lived off of welfare; there was no money in it.

I knew this couldn't be true but I was influenced by these points and hesitant to follow my musical ambitions. When the time came to decide about college, I wanted to attend music school and earn my degree in music, but my parents pushed me into a different path. I had talents for the visual arts so it was decided I would become a graphic designer or an architect. This led to my spending two years at Cornell University where I was unhappy, but I excelled in my studies. Music was pulling at me the whole time. Years later, I did attend music school. I can see why my parents felt the way they did, and I'm even appreciative for what they did, because I learned valuable skills and knowledge at Cornell, while proving my academic abilities. When it came to doing music as a career, I was eventually forced to fight for what I believed in.

As I consider my plans at that tender age, I can see how misguided I was about the world, and particularly about the music business. Ah, the folly of youth! I had this idea that somehow the word "commercial" when applied to music was bad, even evil. Music created for a commercial market meant the artist was "selling out." Art and commerce were mutually exclusive. I had no idea what was really involved with making a living at music. I had this idealistic image of myself playing on stage to thousands of adoring fans, and that was about all I had. Looking back, I see clearly how I was in denial that music is a business, or that a music industry exists. My dream of being a professional musician would be miraculously fulfilled when some magical entity swooped down and handled everything in my life so I could just play my guitar. If only I knew then what I know now!

It seems I was not the only one who believed this. There are plenty of stories about legendary musicians who were taken advantage of financially by their managers and record companies, signing away their future royalties to nefarious individuals who stepped in with a contract. Musicians and artists during this time were naïve, and the lawsuits sprouted like mushrooms later on after they came to realize how badly they were cheated. In most cases it was too late to recover any of their stolen assets. Even Paul McCartney of The Beatles was not savvy enough to stop his (supposed) friend Michael Jackson from snatching up the rights to his song catalogue at an opportune moment. To put it bluntly, musicians and bands lacked business acumen, and there were plenty of sharks ready to eat their lunch.

Eventually, musicians started to get wise. They got tired of being ripped off and started to take matters into their own hands. They started to learn about business. Today, conservatories, colleges, and universities understand that they need to train musicians in the artistry of business. *The skills needed to get the job are not the same skills needed to do the job.* It took me some time to warm to this idea, and I experienced a series of epiphanies that led to me fully embracing it.

Derek Sivers, the founder of CD Baby, musician, book author, and TED speaker, summed it up nicely in a recent blog post (bolding is his):

Shed your money taboos.

Everyone has weird mental associations with money. They think the only way to make money is to take it away from others. They think that charging for your art means it was insincere, and only for profit.

But after knowing thousands of musicians for over twenty years, I've learned this:

The unhappiest musicians are the ones who avoided the subject of money, and are now broke or need a draining day job. It may sound cool to say money doesn't matter—to say "don't worry about it!"—but it leads to a really hard life. Then ultimately your music suffers, because you can't give it the time it needs, and you haven't found an audience that values it.

The happiest musicians are the ones who develop their value and confidently charge a high price. There's a deep satisfaction when you know how valuable you are, and the world agrees. Then it reinforces itself, because you can focus on being the best artist you can be, since you've found an audience that rewards you for it.

So never underestimate the importance of making money. Let go of any taboos you have about it.

Money is nothing more than a neutral exchange of value. If people give you money, it's proof that you're giving them something valuable in return.

By focusing on making money with your music, you're making sure it's valuable to others, not only to you.

I've had tremendous benefits as a result of finally embracing music as a business. Music has provided me with a living, but perhaps equally or more important, I get to perform with great musicians, travel the world, and share my music with so many others. Accepting and embracing music as a business allows me to achieve the dreams I had as a youth, without having to depend on the intervention of some mythical benefactor. Ironically, I ended up teaching music industry courses at a leading music college, where I get to pass my knowledge and experience on to future generations of musicians.

As a music careerist, I have developed well-defined ideas about how to succeed as a musician. My personal career matrix, which I share in this book, relies on the foundational concept of "multiple income streams." There are some crucial strategies for identifying and realizing these income streams, which I will share with you. I've tested and refined these strategies in my own career, and I've seen them work in the careers of other artists, some who are now quite well known. There is a nexus where music and business intersect, and I sincerely hope my shared experience will help you find that nexus as it applies to your own career.

Music is a business, and the sooner one accepts and embraces this fact, the sooner one is likely to see continued success. No matter where you fit in, knowledge of how our business works will be a key to your future career stability as an artist, performer, manager, marketer, writer, producer, teacher, or whatever you see yourself doing to make your living in the industry. This is a book about music careers, what is available, how to prepare for it, and how to think about it. Nobody is truly unique, but our paths are. There are no better tools than business and entrepreneurship to define and guide your path to a music career, as I have learned firsthand. Now, let's shine a bright light on your path forward as a musician and music industry career practitioner.

CHAPTER 1

The Business of Music
Is Still Business

Being good in business is the most fascinating kind of art. Making money is art and working is art and good business is the best art.
—Andy Warhol, from his book The Philosophy of Andy Warhol (1975)

Art Versus Business Art

When I visited the Andy Warhol museum in Pittsburgh, PA, I was stopped in my tracks by the preceding quote, which is prominently displayed in the entry lobby which leads to the galleries filled with his works. The idea of business as art or *business art* cut very close to my psyche in light of my own musical journey. As a young man I had been terrified of "selling out" by producing music that would be "commercial." My idealism had pulled the wool over my eyes about what it really takes to have a career in music. I suffered from naïve misconceptions and prejudices about the music business and about business in general. Looking back, I saw these misconceptions had kept me from my goals. Standing in the lobby of Andy's museum in Pittsburgh, I finally embraced my true calling as a musician. I saw clearly that to create great music, I would also need to create the business of my music. *The business of music is business.* There is music, and then there is music business. They fit together like a hand in a glove. Warhol's quote made me see that. The music is the product, and the business is everything else that it takes to get the product to the consumer, like marketing, sales, management, finance, branding, products, services, packaging, planning, and organization. Andy Warhol was the consummate organization man, perhaps a quirky CEO, but a CEO nonetheless.

Andy Warhol (1928–1987) came from Pittsburgh, attended Carnegie-Mellon University, became a successful commercial illustrator in the 1950s after moving to New York City, and then became a leading figure in the visual arts movement known as *Pop Art*. He is credited with inventing the slogan "15 minutes of fame" and he was also a movie director and a music producer, producing and managing the influential psychedelic rock group *Velvet Underground* during the 1960s. Today, his paintings sell for millions of dollars.

Years before my epiphany in Pittsburgh, I picked up a copy of *Special Events: Best Practices in Modern Event Management*, a textbook by Certified Special Events Professional (CSEP) Joe Goldblatt (1997). As I leafed through the book, I noticed there was a chapter about music. Written from the perspective of an event planner, music was presented as a subfield of the events business. This made perfect sense to me, since live music is often used at all kinds of events, from weddings to award ceremonies. I had been working as a hired musician at events for years, and it had never occurred to me that I was in the events business. As I read the rest of the book, I couldn't stop thinking about all the other industries that music is a part of.

Music Sectors and Subsectors

Music is everywhere—movies, video games, advertising, sporting events, shopping malls, stores, restaurants, elevators. Every time we hear a song in the background, some musician had to write, arrange, perform, record, publish, and license it. Music, as an industry, has its tendrils in many other industries. Music is not only a subsector of other fields; it also has its own subsectors. Recorded music alone is estimated to be an $18 billion industry globally. The live music and concerts industry is valued at around $13 billion. Then there are music products, such as instruments, amplifiers, microphones, studio recording equipment, and even band uniforms. Music education, music publishing, sheet music, music for films and video games, music for advertising (jingles), music for television, karaoke, and music streaming; music is a sizeable industry as a whole and is incredibly diverse in all its parts. As an industry, music is also projected to grow in the future, as the world economy also expands (See Figure 1.1).

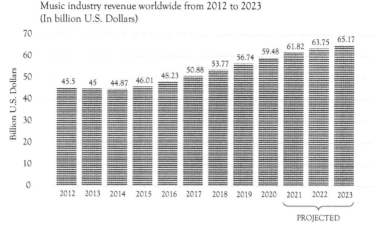

Figure 1.1 *Global music industry revenues*

Like all businesses, music is competitive. There is no easy business, or everyone would be doing it! Everything about being in business is difficult, but that doesn't mean it's complicated. As we begin to describe the music industry as a sector, and as a subsector of other industries, and as we examine further the subsectors within our industry, you will see the layers unfold. It's a fascinating business, with seemingly endless opportunities to innovate. It's also a fun business—at least I've always felt this way about it. If you love music and care about bringing music to the world, you should also love the music business. There's no reason not to.

Diverse Income Streams: Music Careerism

I used this idea of sectors and subsectors to design and develop my own professional music career. My framework is as follows. Combining my talents and skill as a writer, performer, producer, business executive, and educator, I earn my living by doing a combination of all these things concurrently. Taken together, they create a stream of income to support my living costs. While any one pursuit might not provide me with enough total income, in combination they do. I call this concept *multiple income streams* or *diverse income streams*. My analogy works this way: each activity provides a *stream* of earnings; together the streams turn into a *river* (of money) that flows into the *lake*, which is my bank account.

This concept was useful for my own career, and would later lead me to designing my own career matrix, as I will show you at the end of Chapter 2. My job title, or occupation, might be listed as *musician, producer,* or *educator* based on what I am doing at the moment. I call this concept *music careerism*. I could call myself a *music careerist*. Since most wouldn't understand what this means, I normally just tell people I'm a musician.

Revenue Streams and Trends

This book helps you identify and learn how to access the many revenue streams for musicians. Since business is characterized by rapid change and constant upheaval, new opportunities and income streams continually appear while others disappear. Artists must look around corners to forecast new trends, adapt, and then move quickly to leverage new opportunities. Since change is all-pervasive and constant, we must plan for it and always innovate, correct course, and execute effectively in the new business environments. This precept applies to all businesses, especially music.

As change continuously unfolds, we should study the markets and look for patterns. For example, the use of music for visual media has been a growth area for many years. From 1999 to 2020, sales fell from physical copies of recordings, digital downloads came and went, and finally, streaming came into wide use, boosting revenues again.

Performing rights organizations (PROs) collect royalties from music used in television, movies, videogames, and advertising, which is a highly complex task. There is no central clearinghouse for collections of all royalties (yet), so performers and composers rely on the various organizations to collect royalties for the use of their music. As sales from recorded music fell, artists worked to replace that income, from sources such as licensing and concertizing.

Recently, new legislation in the U.S. Congress sought to protect musicians' rights. The Music Modernization Act of 2018 (MMA) attempts to update copyright laws in the United States to apply to the digital age. At the end of this chapter, I'll discuss this further.

As far as future trends go, the use of *blockchain technology* holds a promise for better tracking of music revenues, but is likely a decade or more in the future as of this writing. It's important to pay careful attention to the changes occurring in the music business, to discern and stay on top of trends. Nobody can see the future, but that doesn't prevent us from trying to look around the corner to see what might be coming.

Monetize Your Music, Expand Your Business

Musicians find ways to monetize their music and image beyond recorded music and performances. Like many other female artists, pop star Katy Perry has perfume, shoes, clothes, and makeup lines, as does Rihanna. Although Jay-Z cut his teeth as a rapper, the bulk of his income comes from non-musical ventures. He owns a clothing line, and he's expanded into sports management, founding a high-end boutique agency and earning certification to represent athletes to Major League Baseball and the National Basketball Association. On a smaller scale, independent musicians and bands often earn the bulk of their revenues from selling *merch*, short for merchandise—T-shirts, hats, and other items—before and after their shows.

Many accomplished musicians find careers in teaching. Music education is part of the music industry, though not everyone would immediately recognize it as such. There are celebrity music professors, and a good number of session musicians and orchestra performers also teach privately or at a school or university. There are online courses and subscriptions to music tutorials. Don't ever let anyone tell you there is no money in teaching. It's not unusual to find millionaire professors at top schools.

Then there's the musical instruments business, music software, music production and engineering, sound design, karaoke...when we combine all aspects of the music business we start to see a vibrant industry offering wonderful career opportunities for so many. Music is a sustainable engine of economic activity which for the most part doesn't use excessive raw materials or degrade the environment. Music has the power to reach across cultures, languages, and borders. As famous guitarist and composer Frank Zappa once said: "Art is making something out of nothing, and selling it."

Intellectual Property

The legal framework for music (in the United States) was originally proscribed by the Constitution. Clause eight says: "Congress shall have power to promote the progress of science and useful arts, by securing for limited times to authors and inventors the exclusive right to their respective writings and discoveries." Over the years, Congress has passed laws to protect these rights of creators, most recently the *Music Modernization Act of 2018*, which was passed by a unanimous vote. (*Disclaimer:* I am not a lawyer and therefore cannot dispense legal advice.) Musicians don't need to be trained in law to understand their rights to ownership of their *intellectual property* (IP). These rights are covered by copyrights (literally: the right to copy), sometimes called *soft IP,* versus the patents protecting inventions, known as *hard IP.* Whether soft IP or hard IP, the laws protecting ownership of rights to revenues from IP are very similar, and protect creators from infringement and outright theft.

Professional musicians and others in the music industry should understand how to protect their IP, register and publish a work, get a copyright, license to others, and properly calculate and distribute earnings from their works. While these things are not especially difficult to understand, artists usually retain a qualified entertainment attorney to ensure that laws are adhered to, and the application of the laws and their own understanding of them are thorough and up to date. As with most laws, there are many areas that are open to interpretation. As just one example, there is currently a split in the U.S. federal courts between the 6th and 9th Circuits (Nashville and California, respectively), about how much of a previous work from another artist can be used in a digital sample without compensating the original artist. This split will eventually be settled by the Supreme Court, but to date nobody has yet brought a case on the matter to the highest court.

Copyright protection and payment of royalties can get a bit complicated. For example, a recording or video of a work has a separate copyright from the composition of the work. Copyrights on recordings are sometimes called *mechanicals* or *master license* and may be shared by the producer, engineer, recording label, or others involved with the recording process. Who gets what is decided by special written agreements which are not always properly in place. Disputes over ownership of recorded music have led to numerous legal battles which have often served mainly to enrich entertainment attorneys. Additional layers of complexity may come into the picture when commercialization of a work occurs globally, as each country may be governed by a different set of laws, and there is no central clearinghouse to keep track of all proceeds from musical works. As mentioned earlier, blockchain technology seems to have the potential to change this, but any solution is still years in the future.

Protecting legal rights of artists through publishing, licensing, and syndication deals can feel daunting for the uninitiated, but what you need to know isn't limitless, and the knowledge is accessible. Since change is constant, even the professionals struggle to keep on top of how things are handled with their music rights. Performing Rights Organizations (PROs) such as ASCAP, BMI, and SESAC help composers, songwriters, arrangers, and producers understand the law and collect their royalties. We will discuss music publishing, licensing, and syndication in more specific detail later on.

Music Modernization Act of 2018

The Music Modernization Act of 2018 was the first major legislation to affect music royalties passed since the Copyright Act of 1976. If you consider how much has changed since 1976 in how music is created, sold, and distributed, new legislation was long overdue. It's notable that this law passed both houses of Congress without a single opposing vote. The law regulates how musicians are paid from digital sales and streaming, and sets up a clearinghouse for mechanical rights for engineers and producers. It also affects how royalties are paid for music produced before 1972. While there was unanimous support for the law's passage from musicians and creators, not all the music labels and distributors were happy, since the law potentially impacts their revenue streams.

The new law makes it easier for songwriters to get paid for their work, creates a clearinghouse for digital mechanical royalties called the Mechanical Licensing Collective (MLC), funnels new money to older "legacy" artists who weren't getting paid for streaming, increases streaming royalties by changing the way they are calculated, decreases the portion of payments that never reach rightful recipients by creating a database using new technology, expands royalty rights for producers, and helps songwriters and composers recoup money they lost during transition from sales to streaming. Besides the welcome fact that the law will increase cash flows to artists and musicians, it's remarkable that this legislation passed unanimously, as it was one of the very few policy initiatives where a divided congress could reach bipartisan agreement.

Now that we have an idea of the scope of the music industry, and some of the business challenges, let's focus on how to create a viable career in music. There are many kinds of potential music careers, as we've seen. As you read, keep an open mind and consider where and how you might fit in.

Action Step:

Write your key takeaways from this chapter:

1. What did you learn about music as a business?
2. Name some sectors of the music industry that interest you.
3. What do you want to remember or apply when it comes to your own music business aspirations?

CHAPTER 2

Developing Your Music Career

Music Career Planning: Early Years

Most musicians arrive at the idea of a career in music from experiences with performing, often as a child. When this is the case, we may acquire a musical instrument and imitate the sounds we hear. Voice is considered an instrument, so singing might also be part of our initial exploration into creating music. Our early natural abilities bring positive reinforcement (applause) from others. This feels good, so we keep doing it.

Experiencing the self-satisfaction of learning new skills, we might then take lessons with a teacher, who gives further reinforcement and guidance. As our continued learning requires greater effort, we begin to understand the relationship between effort and progress. We might then apply an even greater effort. This is all typical of the early learning stages for musicians.

As we grow and mature, we become aware of the musical competition and realize that achieving a successful career as a performer might not be so easy. This may or may not discourage us from further pursuing music as a career. We might also be dissuaded from our musical ambitions by disapproving parents or family members, as I was. After all, most people view music as a hobby, or avocation, rather than a calling to a career, or a vocation. They have good reasons for doing so, but to be fair, there is no career that is "easy." If there were, everyone would be doing it. Also to be fair, there are other kinds of careers that are likely more attainable for the average person than becoming a professional musician.

As we aspiring musicians continue to study and progress, we come into contact with others in the music industry. We may see there are other jobs in the music industry besides performing. If we have the benefit of a good counselor, or a mentor, we might explore various nonperformer roles. Music industry programs in college float the idea of working as a talent scout, a booking agent, a publicist, an audio engineer, music educator, a producer, and so on. There are in fact many, many roles in music that are not directly related to performing. Throughout this book you will find examples and descriptions of some of these roles. For now, a sample list includes:

Music-Related Careers

- Arranger
- Producer
- Orchestrator
- Composer
- Jingle writer
- Songwriter
- Transcriber
- Conductor
- Film composer
- Film arranger/adapter
- Music copyist
- Jazz composer
- Music publisher
- Music critic
- MIDI technician
- Programmer
- Performing synthesist
- Music sequencer
- Sound designer
- Music editor
- Music supervisor
- Film conductor
- Film music orchestrator
- Synthesis specialist
- Theme specialist
- Choir director
- Music minister
- Private instructor
- Musicologist
- Editor (print music publishing)
- Educator/teacher
- MIDI engineer
- Music director
- Program director
- Live sound engineer
- Recording engineer
- Mastering engineer
- Studio director/manager
- Music therapist
- Vocal/instrumental soloist
- College/conservatory/university music educator
- Secondary school music teacher
- Elementary school music teacher
- Session musician
- General business musician
- Performing artist
- Orchestra/group member
- Background vocalist
- Floor show band member
- Music blogger
- Lyricist
- Music journalist

- Music publicist
- Performing singer-song-writer
- Staff /freelance songwriter
- Personal manager
- Project manager
- Advertising executive
- Booking agent
- Business manager
- Field merchandiser
- Disc jockey (DJ)
- Tour manager
- Entertainment attorney
- Record label executive
- Talent scout (A&R)
- Label marketing manager
- Stage manager
- Tech (guitar, drums, bass, keys)
- Contest administrator
- Curriculum specialist
- Music school administrator
- Concert promoter
- Social media manager
- Product demonstrator
- Cruise director
- Lighting designer
- Art director
- Music software developer
- Music group travel agent

This list is not meant to be exhaustive, and as the industry develops, new roles will come into existence as others fade away.

The Gig Mentality

Although full-time jobs can be found in the music industry, many musicians work independently on a *freelance* basis, especially during initial stages of career building. The word *gig* originates from the Baroque period of classical music, originally spelled *gigue* (French) and used to describe a musical song form used for accompanying dancers at a festive event, such as a royal ball. Starting in the 20th century, a gig became the parlance of musicians and is still used to describe a paying music job or performance, usually with a contract. In the 21st century, the word gig entered the lexicon of the masses, as in the *gig economy* where workers were retained on an "as-needed" basis, relieving employers of the necessity and higher cost of maintaining long-term employment arrangements. The gig economy has some negative connotations (lack of job security), but many see a more positive outcome and appreciate having flexibility to choose the days and hours they wish to work.

Musicians are uniquely prepared to survive and thrive in the gig economy, as they've always dealt with finding itinerant work on a somewhat haphazard basis. I've sometimes used the word *journeyman* to describe the work I do as a gigging musician: traveling the world with my tools (my guitars) to do highly skilled freelance work where and when it's needed.

This brings me to my next topic: To succeed, musicians need specialized technical skills and highly specialized knowledge. As in any profession, critical study and sustained preparation is required. One needs a body of general knowledge, plus specialized information and skills for each kind of musical job. Whether through formal education or self-study (or both), the serious music careerist must work long and hard to gain skills. (Professional networking is also a crucial skill; we will return to this subject in a later chapter.) Some roles might require certification, such as a music therapist or public school music teacher. This means passing an exam. As author Malcolm Gladwell has stated, it takes about 10,000 hours to get really good at anything. That translates to 20 hours a week, for 10 years, more or less.

Action Steps:
1. Look at the prior list of jobs, and select any that interest you.
2. Write them down.
3. Write a list of skills and preparation that are required for each.

Self-Assessment and SMART Goals

As we consider possible roles in the music industry, we should undertake a self-assessment to take inventory of our skills, likes, and dislikes, to reveal which roles could be a good fit. They say "knowledge is power." Self-knowledge can be powerful indeed. A series of questions should be asked and answered about your likes and dislikes, your background and current skills, and what will make you happy in your professional life and career. These aren't easy questions, and it could take some time to answer them (Figure 2.1). Your goal is to gain a deeper understanding of what motivates you in your career, while looking at the past, present, and future.

This self-assessment will lead you to setting some goals. (A goal is a specific dream with a timeline.) Goals might include getting (or completing) your education, learning a specific skill, developing your repertoire,

Music Industry Self-Assessment Exercise

Knowledge is power, and self knowledge is crucial in all aspects of business and life. In this exercise, we will explore how you might view yourself as a music industry professional, based on your background, experiences, and preferences, while also taking into account your own career and life goals.

There are no right or wrong answers. All questions should be answered as completely and honestly as possible. Answers should be in short paragraph form. Take enough time to consider each question carefully before writing the answers. If a question doesn't seem to apply to you, you can write N/A (Not Applicable) as an answer, but most questions should be relevant to you in some way if you think about it carefully.

After completing, save this document where you can retrieve it easily. Later, you can refer back to your answers to remind you of your motivations, purpose, and perceived strengths or weaknesses.

> **NOTE:** For our purposes, "work" refers to your work in the music or music-related industries. If it makes sense, you can include other kinds of work you are engaged with (such as a "day-job" or a non-music profession). Try to be as specific as you can with your answers.

1. What are your main interests, outside of your school or work? How might these interests play into your role in the music industry? Have you been involved with any specific causes in the past? What kinds of hobbies do you take part in? What is your level of involvement in any causes or hobbies?
2. Which parts of your work do you like most? What are the least favorite aspects of your work? Isolate your most and least favorite parts and describe why you like or dislike them.
3. Identify the aspects of being in music that seem most interesting and fulfilling to you. Can you describe your dream career?
4. Are there any causes or charities that you are passionate about? Do you do any volunteer work or donate to charities?
5. List all your educational and employment experiences including where you worked or studied, what you did, how long, etc. (you may include a professional resume or CV.)
6. Describe any technical skills, processes, techniques, equipment, etc. that you have studied or mastered.
7. List any familiarity with products, services, or business endeavors you have gained through formal or informal experience, education, training, work, or family background.
8. Describe your ideal music industry role (job), including your main responsibilities, level of success, income, and how being in the role might interact with or enhance the kind of lifestyle you envision for yourself.
9. Describe your management style. Are you collaborative, or authoritative? Are you more detail-oriented or like to see the bigger picture? Can you delegate?
10. What do you believe to be your strongest and weakest points, both professionally and personally?

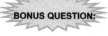 **BONUS QUESTION:**   Describe your network. Who is in it, and how do you go about networking?

Figure 2.1 Self-assessment exercise

moving to a new city, writing a certain number of songs, getting work as a private teacher, getting a day job, taking lessons with a certain person... really just about anything you aspire to do can become a goal. The important thing is that the goals are realistic, time based, and specific.

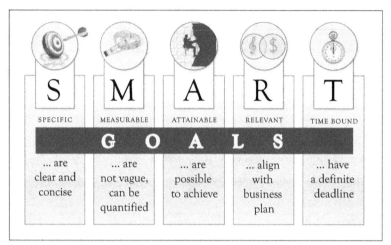

Figure 2.2 S.M.A.R.T goals chart

We might consider using the SMART goals acronym (Figure 2.2). This states that all goals should be:

- Specific: Know exactly what you intend to achieve.
- Measurable: Have concrete evidence of achievement.
- Attainable: Have the time and resources to achieve.
- Relevant: Make sure the goal aligns with your purpose and desires.
- Time bound: Have a timeline and hold yourself accountable.

It's important to take the thought and time to write all your goals down. I recommend you make a clear list of your goals and post it where you'll see it every day, such as on a wall in your office, bedroom, kitchen, or bathroom. Keeping your goals foremost in mind is important as you go through your daily tasks, to remind you of the important actions you must take to accomplish the goals you have set. Setting goals is the main purpose of the career self-assessment exercise and is a necessary step to structuring your daily work in ways that bring you closer to achieving your goals. It's easy to get sidetracked by urgent matters that are not important, and to procrastinate with the important things that aren't really urgent.

Career Matrix

Early on, I found it helpful to design a career matrix for myself. I continue to refer to it as I diligently work toward my goals. The career matrix provides a way to visualize your path forward. My own matrix takes the shape of a triangle or pyramid, which was inspired by sources such as Maslow's Hierarchy and John Wooden's Pyramid of Success. I just like triangles for some reason. Figure 2.3 is my own version of the career matrix.

At each corner of the triangle I put one of my three main areas of expertise: performance, business, and education. Performance is at the top because my musical abilities legitimize the other things I do. Next, I listed revenue-generating activities alongside each area.

In between each area of expertise, I added other activities that combined skills from each primary area, and these became secondary combined areas of competency (not less important than the primary areas, though).

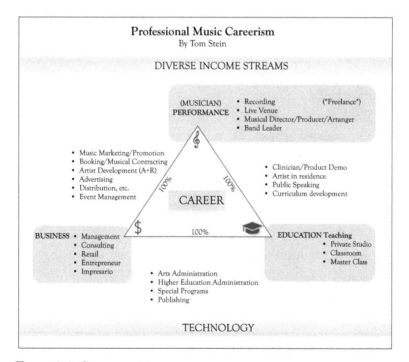

Figure 2.3 Career matrix

For example, between performance and education I wrote down "curriculum development" and "artist-in-residence." Combining business and performance, I added "booking/music contracting" and "artist development." Between education and business I put "arts administration." Underneath it all, I have "technology," which supports all the areas.

I call my matrix *Professional Music Careerism* because it was the title I felt best describes what it shows. My occupation is *Musician*, which encompasses all of these activities.

Your career matrix could take many forms: a square, a circle with items inside and outside, a line with items above or below, or a 3D representation.

Some people use a mind-mapping program or write their career goals on index cards to arrange on a table. I have used online presentation tools like Prezi and PowerPoint to create matrixes, but the original one I created years ago was drawn by hand on a sheet of paper. Think about what your own career matrix might look like and experiment with creating it. A career matrix can help you to define and visualize your music career.

Action Steps:

1. Choose your tool (mind-mapping software, index cards, Prezi or PowerPoint, or paper).
2. Write your main areas of expertise down. You want to end up with a manageable number, but you can write more to start with and narrow it down later. These could be performer, songwriter, producer, educator, or any other combination from Table 2.1 or that you can imagine.
3. Pick a shape that works for you. Although I personally prefer triangles, you can choose another shape. Use your imagination!
4. Now add your expertise areas to your matrix and write down your professional activities for each area.

CHAPTER 3

The Artist as Entrepreneur

As a young musician, I didn't fully understand the meaning of the word "business" as it related to music. As I described in my introduction, my belief that art and commerce are mutually exclusive held me back and kept me from realizing my goals. Once I started questioning my strongly held beliefs, I was able to move forward.

When it comes to the business of music, it's wise to question your most strongly held beliefs and seek new information about them. You can take that kind of critical thinking ability and apply it to anything in your life. In this chapter, I offer suggestions for how to think about the music business in new and different ways. You may be pleasantly surprised to see how you are already well prepared to become an entrepreneurial musician (sometimes called a *musipreneur*) with the skills you have now and how you can learn to direct your thinking patterns into more productive channels.

Artist-entrepreneurship can be taught and learned. In some ways, being an entrepreneur in the music industry is no different from being an entrepreneur in any other industry. But in other specific and meaningful ways, the artist-entrepreneur will need to harness their creativity and intelligence to leverage opportunities unique to our industry.

Learning about marketing, sales, and finance are important, but there are myriad skills and capabilities for artist-entrepreneurs to investigate and learn. For example, if you plan to earn money from giving live concerts, you would be wise to learn everything you possibly can about how to successfully produce a concert. We use the terms *professional music* and *music industry* to refer to the broad field of music business that draws on a wide range of skills to create something of value, which can then be marketed and sold to generate revenue. Revenue is a synonym for money, or income. If you don't have revenue, you don't have a business.

By the way, I use the terms "music business" and "music industry" interchangeably throughout the book. I like to use the term *music industry* to include all the aspects of being in the music business. If you start a business to provide a solution or product and fill a demand in the marketplace, you are an entrepreneur. *Artist-entrepreneurship* describes the processes and techniques artists and musicians use to achieve independent business success in their chosen field.

You Are Already Prepared

Let's get right to the point of this discussion. If the business of music is business, then we need to learn how business works. Although luck is always a factor, business is not mysterious. Anyone can learn it if they are willing to apply themselves. If you can learn music, you can learn business.

Fortunately, musicians already have skills that cross over to entrepreneurship. I call them meta-skills, because they can be applied to many different situations.

Let's examine some of these meta-skills:

- Creative thinking
- Problem solving
- Disciplined learning
- Executive leadership
- Soft skills (emotional intelligence, interpersonal skills)
- Collaboration and teamwork
- Communication skills
- Stamina
- Focus
- Persistence and drive

Action Step:
How about you? What are some of the skills from the aforementioned list that you already have? List them here:
Not sure? Keep reading.

Understanding Creative Thinking: Right Brain Versus Left Brain

Students who study music tend to achieve better grades in other academic subjects in school. The ancient Greeks treated music as one of the required subjects to be studied by all students, along with reading, writing, and arithmetic. Harvard professor in cognitive science Howard Gardner included musical intelligence as one of the eight kinds of intelligence in his famous theory of multiple intelligences. Music has been shown to have a positive effect on brain development in young people by increasing neuroplasticity and enhancing creative and analytical thinking skills.

Musicians who have been highly trained in the creative aspects of music will usually have strong deductive skills and creative abilities in other areas. Connective thinking, using associations between disparate ideas, is

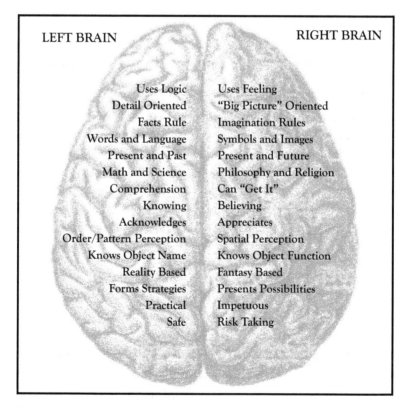

LEFT BRAIN	RIGHT BRAIN
Uses Logic	Uses Feeling
Detail Oriented	"Big Picture" Oriented
Facts Rule	Imagination Rules
Words and Language	Symbols and Images
Present and Past	Present and Future
Math and Science	Philosophy and Religion
Comprehension	Can "Get It"
Knowing	Believing
Acknowledges	Appreciates
Order/Pattern Perception	Spatial Perception
Knows Object Name	Knows Object Function
Reality Based	Fantasy Based
Forms Strategies	Presents Possibilities
Practical	Impetuous
Safe	Risk Taking

Figure 3.1 Left brain–right brain

a hallmark of creative ability, and research has shown that the most successful entrepreneurs all have very strong creative abilities. Music is made up of complex patterns based on mathematics, so musicians are usually good at math and at recognizing patterns in complex series of numbers. Music uses both the left brain (analytical; logical; sequential) and right brain (intuitive; holistic and artistic ways of thinking) (Figure 3.1).

Don't worry if you aren't great at all these things. Nobody is great at everything. Thinking creatively, or *outside the box*, and analytically, or linearly, are important meta-skills that can be applied to starting and operating any kind of business.

Problem Solving

You solve complex problems every day whether you're figuring out how to play a difficult passage on an instrument, writing a complicated orchestral score, or using sophisticated computer software to make recordings. We musicians must learn to analyze complex problems, identify obstacles, and use feedback to create effective strategies for solving the problems.

Problem solving is second nature to musicians and a key strength for entrepreneurs. When starting a business, you will have to solve for unknowns. Although business schools use models and case studies to teach students about the way business works, learning on the job gives you real-time experience. Solving unknown and unpredictable problems is an important capability for the entrepreneur, and musicians have specialized training and experience that helps them to understand and solve complex problems.

While we are discussing problems, I'd like to tell you that *problem* is a word I avoid using. Having a problem implies that there is some solution. Not every problem will have a solution. I prefer using the word *issue* instead of problem. Regardless, artist-entrepreneurs are constantly solving for the unknown.

Develop and use your meta-skill of observing how you solve the many problems you regularly face. Self-understanding can be very helpful when deciding the best course of action in turbulent times, and you want to avoid reacting based on emotions. There are times when it's wise to follow your gut feeling, and other times where you should take a few steps back and analyze what's really happening, so you can act proactively, instead of just reacting.

Many issues we face in business relate to interpersonal communications. It's crucial to grow your understanding of psychology, and especially organizational behavior, the psychology of group dynamics. Working in high-level performing musical groups, such as a band or an orchestra, is a great way to learn about leadership and conflict resolution. The interpersonal skills I learned by playing in and leading bands as a conductor are so helpful to me in business. Most problems in organizations arise from errors in communication and organization, and it is always management's fault, since they are the ones in charge. Ultimately, learning to solve problems in management means learning to solve problems with people.

Action Step:
What are some of the problems you solve in music already? List some here.

Disciplined Learning

Mastering a musical instrument takes disciplined practice and study. Setting hard goals and working consistently and diligently to reach them should feel familiar to the master musician. Musicians must be committed to continuous learning, and this applies equally to learning skills in business. While nothing about business is really easy, a musician has a better chance of mastering all aspects of business, especially in the music industry, compared to someone without the habit of disciplined learning. Musicians intuitively and quickly learn from empirical knowledge. Observation, feedback, and problem solving all lead to disciplined ways of learning new material.

Young people in particular benefit from neuroplasticity, meaning that their still-developing brain can quickly forge new pathways between neurons. This is why people always say it is easiest to learn a new language when you are young. (Music is also an international language.) Really, it is easier to learn *anything* when you are young. As a young person, if you set your mind and heart on learning business, you will assuredly succeed.

Keep an open mind and stay curious. Seek out the best resources for your learning, decide to commit the time to learn, and then make a disciplined and honest effort. The rewards will always be worth it.

Executive Leadership

Leaders in business must create a vision and mission with input from those tasked with doing the work needed to reach the goals. Leaders must work to cast the vision, assemble teams, communicate effectively, set expectations, establish direction, and build cohesion in the team. Leaders need to establish structure, balance risk, and make decisions. Running a band, directing recording studio sessions, producing concerts, and conducting an orchestra are all excellent ways to learn executive leadership skills needed to succeed in business.

While the words "leadership" and "management" are sometimes used interchangeably, leadership implies a more inspirational and motivational role than management, which is seen as coordinating the use of resources and people. Good leaders need followers, and to get them they must project a coherent vision that others can integrate with their own personal goals, while building high levels of trust in their capabilities and loyalties. Strong leadership is a skill in high demand, and developing your leadership acumen should be a high priority, as it will contribute to your chances of success in anything you do. Strong leaders also make good followers and enhance the success of any organization.

Soft Skills (Emotional Intelligence, Interpersonal Skills)

Leading teams in an organization also requires exceptional people skills. As mentioned before, leaders need capabilities in psychology and using motivational techniques to lead a smooth running team. Knowing how to listen and developing strong interpersonal skills are important to eliciting buy-in from all members of a team.

Getting all team members on the same page pulling together to meet the mandate requires important soft skills that musicians learn from playing in ensembles and orchestras. Experienced musicians have studied the leadership skills of others, worked on teams, and experienced the joy of working together with others to achieve difficult goals. This makes them natural leaders. They need not only intelligence (IQ), but also *emotional intelligence* (EQ).

Collaboration and Teamwork

Music is a collaborative art form. The ensemble experience is all about working together with other musicians and artists to create a beautiful sound. This always requires some give and take. Most musicians are intuitively effective at collaboration, because they have to be. Collaboration and teamwork are habits that translate effectively to the world of business. Even music composers, technologists, engineers, software developers, and others who spend much time working alone will need to collaborate with others to get their product or service to the end user in the marketplace.

At the very least, finding a good accountant and lawyer is a prerequisite for success in business, because taxes must be paid and contracts must be legal. Finding the people for your team takes patience, diligence, and special skills for evaluating potential team members' abilities, reliability, and motivation.

Action Steps:
1. Consider who will be part of your team and make a list.
2. Research entertainment lawyers and accountants and make a list of at least three of each to consider.

Communication Skills

Whether it's communication with other musicians on stage, or with the audience, musicians are natural communicators. They are sensitive to *body language* and have been trained to interpret body and facial cues from a conductor or from other musicians. Good musicians are often strong verbal communicators with a powerful vocabulary and strong persuasive abilities. They know how to use nonverbal communication, or body language. Some musicians use *power poses* to get a point across or prepare to put on a performance. Harvard psychology professor and TED speaker

Amy Cuddy has shared her research on power poses with the world, and I recommend you investigate her work. Rock band front-vocalists like Mick Jagger of the Rolling Stones are experts at power poses.

While writing well or speaking in public presents a challenge to most people, musicians have learned to deal with performance anxiety. Musicians and artists make outstanding communicators in business. Skillful communications and group bonding dynamics are important meta-skills where expert musicians have an advantage.

Stamina

Stamina is defined as "the ability to sustain prolonged physical or mental effort" and is synonymous with endurance or perseverance. Learning to play a musical instrument certainly requires stamina. A musician who has learned to play an instrument well knows that one has to keep at something over a long period to truly master it. You might even call it *stick-to-it-iveness*.

Musicians know they can learn difficult things if they put in the time. They also know how to use their mind to overcome any physical discomfort or fatigue while playing. Malcom Gladwell, in his book *Outliers: The Story of Success*, used The Beatles' experience playing long gigs in Hamburg prior to their breakthrough to fame as an example for his 10,000 hours theory. Launching a business requires grueling work, and persistence and endurance are required.

Focus

Along with stamina comes the need to maintain *focus*. The definition of stamina mentions prolonged mental effort, and this is where focus is required. Maintaining extreme focus is required during a musical performance. If the mind is allowed to wander for even a moment, a mistake can occur. The amount of focus needed to perform a difficult piece of music can be compared to the level of focus a surgeon needs to perform an operation, or a pilot needs to land a large jetliner. Even though lives may not be at stake for the musician, the pressure is still on to maintain unwavering focus, if only to preserve the musician's reputation.

Persistence and Drive

Sometimes it takes a lot of no's to get to yes. Bouncing back from constant rejection is an important skill for musicians. Some Broadway performers go to more than a hundred auditions every year, in order to land a single part. Musicians learn to harness the sting of rejection to increase their energy, keep moving forward, and learn something from each failure to help them compete even harder. Success in any aspect of music or life often requires *persistence* and *drive*. Fall down seven times, get up eight, as the well-known Japanese proverb says.

At this point you should start to see a pattern: The artistic skills musicians develop naturally are applicable in the world of business. I use the word *artistry* to describe how we apply our previous musical knowledge and training in new areas. Artistry is yet another meta-skill.

All of these music-related capabilities, traits, and meta-skills transfer to the world of business, and accomplished musicians have a real business learning advantage by having them at their disposal. For the nonmusician, this doesn't mean that business skills can't be learned in other ways. Neither are these the only skills that musicians bring to the table. Any fully trained consummate professional should be well prepared to build a career in the music industry should they choose to transfer their skills over to the area of music business. We will return to the application of these skills in later chapters with more concrete examples of how you can newly leverage your own current business-relevant expertise.

Action Steps:
1. List any additional skills you learned from music here.
2. Write down how each of these skills could be helpful to you in your music industry career.

CHAPTER 4

Business Planning and Development: Early Stages

In the "old days," artists viewed the business side of music as being separate from the music. They hoped or expected that someone else would manage their business for them, so they could be free to just create. In the current digital environment of direct-to-fan and viral social media marketing, that's an outdated model. The artist is now fully responsible for the business side of their artistic career. As you will see, what is needed is a deliberate mindset—a set of principles, attitudes, and ways of thinking—which, together, will prepare the musician to compete in the music industry.

Andy Warhol's life as a highly successful artist exemplified the deliberate use of creative faculties to succeed in the business of art. His approach, or mindset, showed the kind of entrepreneurial thinking I believe is crucial to career success in the music industry. We will address the kinds of thinking and thought processes that enable success in any industry later on. For now, let's turn our attention to the topic of business planning.

Some artists might prefer to ignore the realities of the business and focus only on what they want to express with their art. This might be possible if you don't need to earn a living with your art but carries with it the risk of obscurity. As Andy Warhol proved, and I discussed in the previous chapter, your creative powers can be readily applied to success in business art. After thinking deeply about your own unique skills and experience and how they might lend themselves to launching and running your music career, the next step is to express your music career idea in the form of a business plan.

Why Write a Business Plan?

Writing your business plan can be a great place to start exploring and developing your meta-skills, while taking a cold hard look at potential opportunities and obstacles. Creating the plan can be an incredible and fun journey. After all, you're creating your future life's work and expressing your music career ideas in a new format. You will also carefully research the market for your music. For now, let's examine the reasons why you will need a business plan.

The creation of a business plan does much more than provide a plan for your music business. As you progress with it, you will work to identify all opportunities and obstacles to success, and then create strategies to overcome the obstacles while leveraging the opportunities. You will be forced to articulate your specific goals in writing and consider the timeline for achieving those goals. Among other things, a business plan will help you:

- Define your business;
- Understand your target market;
- Define your products and services;
- Outline your go-to-market strategy;
- Create an operating plan;
- Assemble a team;
- Project future outcomes.

Writing a business plan is a science and art. The science part involves researching your market and structuring the plan in a formal way that communicates your idea effectively to potential partners, employees, clients, and investors. The art of writing a business plan is in describing and creating the products and services your business will provide, envisioning the branding materials and organizational structure, sizing up the competition, and coming up with the strategies that will ultimately allow you to succeed.

This may seem a tall order if you're not steeped in business. However, with a little guidance, you can quickly learn to embrace the methodologies of business planning. Writing a great business plan is not rocket science, and it isn't mystical. Your mission is to figure out how you can best serve your fans, customers, clients, partners, and employees in a sustainable way.

Without revenue there is no business. You must earn money in order to stay alive. This is true even if you are a nonprofit. We use terms like *monetization, revenue enhancement,* and *business development* to describe strategies for getting the money coming into your business. As with any profession, having a grasp on terminology used in the field will be helpful.

Strategies for Success: Identify Opportunities and Obstacles

Writing a business plan encourages you into a way of thinking that might be new to you. You will need to think deeply about what you want to accomplish with your music and career and create projections about the future. This includes scouting for opportunities.

Too many people become lost in their career because they haven't yet learned to recognize opportunities staring them in the face. The ability to see new opportunities is a crucial part of success. For example, Steve Jobs saw in advance that there would be a need for personal computing and created the Macintosh personal computer. Bill Gates saw the opportunity to produce and license the software that would be used on so many computers.

Stock traders and investors look for stocks that are undervalued, so they can buy them and later sell at a higher price. Someone who opens a restaurant believes that hungry customers will walk through the door. Each and every business owner believes there is an opportunity for them to succeed or they wouldn't have started their company. Knowledge is power, and self-knowledge is very powerful indeed. Thinking about how your music will benefit others is a useful exercise. We will also need to think about who these future customers, or fans, will be.

There is usually more than one path to a goal. Many people, when they encounter a serious obstacle to the goal, change the goal rather than changing the path to the goal. There may be a point where it makes sense to change your goals, for example, if you find out they are completely unrealistic or unattainable. But in most cases, we can't know this at the outset, so it's best to investigate ways to get around the roadblocks. Before you dig in deeper here, be sure you've finished the self-assessment step in Chapter 2. Then, keeping in mind our likes, dislikes, strengths, and weaknesses, we'll consider techniques for recognizing new opportunities.

Goals Always Have Obstacles

If something is worth doing, many will do it—or at least try. For example, let's say you have a band and want to go on tour. You also want to get a recording contract and develop a large audience, so you can work full time on your music and make a good living with it. This is a lofty goal, and you know it won't be easy, but you also know that others have done it and are doing it right now. You believe that your music is good enough. If not you, then who? If not now, then when?

Let me ask you a simple question: What do you think is the biggest obstacle to the kind of success you envision for yourself? It's a one-word answer: competition. There is a huge oversupply of talented musicians and a relatively small number of fans. This may vary based on the region you live in or style of music you create, but the music industry as a global business is oversaturated with supply. It's not only other bands or musicians you will be competing with. Entertainment expenditures come out of what is called *disposable income* meaning the money people have left after they pay for necessities, such as housing, clothes, transportation, and food.

Understanding that you are in competition with all these other possible ways people can have fun should lead you to thinking about how you can market yourself to them as an alternative. This means you will need to analyze the competition carefully, focusing on the products and services they offer, their target market, and why you think you can be better than them. To overcome the obstacle of competition, you will need a clear strategy to offer your prospects something better.

Action Steps:
Once you've formulated your goals, the next questions should be:
   1. What can stop you from reaching your goals?
   2. What could you do better?

3. What opportunities do you see?

4. What could you do to remove, or navigate around, obstacles?

What Makes You Different?

Another important question is: What is it about you that makes you different from all the others who do what you do? You can't just say "I'm good" because a lot of people are good. You can't say "I'm me," because others are also authentically themselves. So what is it about you, really, that makes you different?

Pondering this from the perspective of your intended audience eventually results in your *differentiation strategy*; more than just knowing what about you is different, this includes how you intend to let your prospects in on the secret. You will need to have a strong differentiation strategy. We will address this topic more thoroughly when we discuss music marketing.

For now, focus on developing effective visualization techniques for identifying opportunities, learn to predict the obstacles to leveraging those opportunities, and then strategize about how best to overcome the obstacles with a go-to-market strategy.

Keep a Positive Mindset and Guard Against Negative Thinking

Hedge fund billionaire, philanthropist, and author Ray Dalio explains one of his principles:

> The quality of your life ultimately depends on the quality of your decisions, and since work is such a big part of life, you need to make sure that how you spend your work time is aligned with your goals. What's important to you? Being on a fulfilling mission? Making money? Stability? Or excitement and unpredictability? Your answers to these questions may evolve over time, but what's constant is the need to answer them and closely visualize different opportunities to see which path is aligned with the type of life you want. For example, say you're considering whether you want to work for someone else or strike out on your own? You need to visualize closely what your life will be like on each path,

and how each path fits with what you are like. As you do this, make sure to triangulate with people who have succeeded and failed going down each path.

Dalio describes an important tool for visualizing success in any business. Keeping in mind that music is a business, and that all businesses share many principles and techniques, it makes sense to look outside of the music business for even more principles to guide your thinking.

One place we can look is the inspirational literature from the last century, sometimes referred to as "self help," or in academic circles, as *New Thought*. New Thought was a movement among physicists, scientists, religionists, and academics to uncover the mysteries of human consciousness using quasi-scientific methods (and some meta-physics), which began in the late 19th century. In the first half of the 20th century "self-help" books emerged as popular literature. Later, in the 1960s, there was a veritable explosion of these books on the scene. Comedian George Carlin humorously pointed out that "self-help" is a misnomer, since the reader is getting help from the author of the book.

One of the earliest New Thought best-sellers to appear was *How to Win Friends and Influence People,* by Dale Carnegie. Originally published in 1936, it has sold more than 15 million copies worldwide, making it one of the best-selling books of all time. Other best-selling personal development books to come out around the same time included *Think and Grow Rich* by Napoleon Hill, *The Power of Positive Thinking* by Norman Vincent Peale, and later on, books by authors such as Louise Hay, Deepak Chopra, and Dr. Wayne Dyer.

Although they face some valid criticisms, these books became popular in public opinion when first published and they continue to sell well today. One of the main ideas these books all have in common is that the way one thinks is an important indicator and tool for success in business and in life, and that people can exercise some control over their thoughts in order to attract success to themselves.

The authors point out that everything ever accomplished by human beings began with thinking. Therefore, you can affect certain desired outcomes by attending carefully to your thinking. They suggest using affirmations to replace self-doubt and increase confidence, and to use your thinking to positively affect your chances of being successful. In Chapter 15 at the end of the book, we will return to this idea as we investigate the psychology and philosophy of success in greater detail, and apply it to success in the music industry.

Attitudes for Success

Start by looking around you. Who are the people you most admire? They don't need to be in music, they can come from any walk of life. They can be friends, teachers, family, or people you've read about in the news or follow on social media. Start by analyzing them a bit, focusing especially on their life's story and how they came to be in their current situation. What did they do? Why did they do it? No one is truly unique, we all share so many similar attributes as humans. But everyone's path through life is unique.

Action Steps:
1. Take a moment and list the people you admire here. Write the name down of people you admire and then write down what they did and why you think they did it.
2. Answer these questions about them: What role did luck, skill, timing, ambition, or talent play in their success? How do their initial goals and the strategies they used align with your own?
3. As you analyze the approaches others have taken in business, start to ask yourself probing questions about your own situation.

I strongly recommend reading biographies of famous people you admire. This is a great way to absorb the secrets of their success, and study what they did. Reading biographies of successful people is a great way to prepare yourself to recognize opportunities in your own career.

Sometimes you might be able to talk with them directly or even interview them. If you're able to do this, ask them probing questions about their path to success. Look especially for their times of hardship and struggle; failure is always part of the road to success. Analyze how they recovered from their failures, their bad luck, or their mistakes.

For some people the obstacles might lie in their own habits. For example, if you are generally lazy, or afraid to talk to others, that could present an obstacle to success. Looking very hard at yourself is important, and looking at the environment around you is equally important. There will always be a battle with two enemies: the enemy within and the enemy without.

Look for any similarities their story may have to your own, and try to identify with their feelings, attitudes, and approach to goal setting and overcoming obstacles. Pay careful attention to their thought processes.

Action Step:
Write down your ideas about how thinking could affect success or failure. How might these ideas apply to you?

Networking: Who Do You Know?

We've all heard the expression: It's not what you know, it's who you know. More accurately: It's what you can do, who knows you can do it, and who they know with a need for it. As with any profession, networking undeniably plays a key role in success in the music industry. It's true that a chance meeting with someone can change the entire course of your career, and today that chance encounter is more likely to happen online. Effective social media strategies and proper understanding and use of social media marketing analytics should be an important part of how you promote yourself and your personal brand. In Chapter 9 we will examine how to network in the music business much more in-depth.

Social Entrepreneurship

Can music change the way people think about the world they live in? One function of art is to reflect beauty and truth back to society. There's a long history of musicians and entertainers using their fame to advance social causes or peace, from actor and film producer Charlie Chapman to singer Bono of the Irish pop supergroup U2. Sports figures have also taken sides on issues, such as when boxer Muhammad Ali protested the draft during the Vietnam War. More recently, former NFL quarterback Colin Kaepernick has taken a stand against racism and police brutality, at a great cost to his football career.

Many young musicians care deeply about serious problems in the world today, and wonder what, if anything, they could do about it. It's easy to feel helpless in the face of so much suffering; whether it's starving kids or degradation of the environment, disease, crime, homelessness, cruelty to animals, or any of the lengthy laundry list of issues, what can one person do? Well, one person can make a difference. Dr. Martin Luther King, Jr., once said: "If I cannot do great things, I can do small things in a great way." There is a long tradition of musicians and artists advocating for social change and lending support to philanthropic causes.

Music can be a powerful instrument for social change and also for raising awareness of issues among the public. This is true of any art form, but music has an immediate emotional impact with its combination of melody and lyric, harmony and rhythm all working together. Music can worm its way into your psyche and make you feel things that words alone could not. There is a reason that totalitarian political regimes tightly control music, art, and literature through censorship: They know the power of art to change peoples' minds, hearts, and souls. The dictators of the world are just as afraid of artists as they are of guns and tanks. Artists in less-than-free societies often face suppression of their work and even outright persecution by authorities.

Artists certainly have an important role to play in society. Some are purely entertainers, while others use their music to effect change by expressing opinions overtly or through subtler means. For example, during the 1960s in the United States, Folk music, and then Rock and Roll rose to prominence as a form of protest against the Vietnam War and oppressive social mores. Musicians fought back against perceived oppressive societal norms around sexuality, protested against the war, and supported the civil rights movement, giving voice to a generation. Music was a clarion call to action for young idealists, and songs were written about the protests in the streets. Artists are also cultural ambassadors when they perform abroad. Louis Armstrong was known worldwide as America's Jazz Ambassador and for decades had higher name recognition abroad than the U.S. president.

More recently, Hip Hop and Rap music have served to glorify or condemn certain lifestyles, push beliefs (and products) on listeners through the lyrics, or just entertain. Music has often carried a political message, sometimes hidden but often direct. Since art is supposed to be a reflection of society, holding up a mirror to show us who we really are, it makes sense that artists would be outspoken about current issues, although not all are. Many musicians desire not only to make a mark with their music, but also to be a force for good in the world. It is possible to use your music as a tool for change, by drawing attention to injustices or raising awareness of pressing social issues. But it requires some careful thought and planning to be effective. Having the right motivations and methods is key. It's also crucial to study what others have done.

Social Entrepreneurship and Corporate Social Responsibility (CSR)

Entrepreneurs solve problems in the world by starting companies to market and sell products or services that improve people's lives in some way. Social entrepreneurship means using business techniques, approaches, and resources to solve problems in society. Using entrepreneurial approaches can help solve seemingly intractable problems in the world, where other attempts have failed. For example, governments often lack the will or the resources to solve the most serious problems, such as the climate crisis. While there is some disagreement about the exact meaning of the term *social entrepreneurship*, social entrepreneurs start businesses specifically to address urgent needs or to promote social justice. There are as many ways to accomplish this as there are people doing it.

Other terms with similar meanings to social entrepreneurship are "conscious capitalism," "corporate social responsibility (CSR)," "stakeholder capitalism," "experiential marketing," and "values-led business." In 1998 Ben Cohen and Jerry Greenfield, of Ben and Jerry's Ice Cream fame, wrote a book about values-led business, in which they showed how every step of the business process could express and apply positive community values. Companies such as Starbucks, Chobani Yogurt, and Virgin Atlantic focus on treating their employees fairly as a way to give back and to enhance employees' treatment of customers. Newman's Own is a food products company that donates all profits to charity, founded by the late movie actor Paul Newman. Nike and the Ford

Foundation are additional examples of CSR, which address pressing issues in society at large, and support the arts.

Though they operate differently, these companies all share a commitment to giving back to the community in some way. Because of the positive image they project, they attract customers and motivate their employees. They are proof that it's possible to do good in the world while enhancing prospects for business growth and success. There are many examples of pro-social companies that give back to society at large. Activist-minded artists should study these companies to evaluate the effectiveness of their methods.

Celebrity Brand Activism

As mentioned, many artists, pop stars, actors, sports figures, and other celebrities feel a strong need to speak out publicly in support of causes important to them. Whether advocating for political, social, or humanitarian causes, they see their activism as a way to use their fame to make a positive difference and leave behind an enduring legacy. Let's look more closely at this idea.

A celebrity or a musical artist is a brand. People seek to enhance their sense of self-worth through association with brands. This is a psychological reality of which professional marketers are well aware. When an artist or celebrity aligns with a cause, whether social or political, it will always have an effect on the perception of their brand. It is certainly possible to use activism as a way to build your brand as an artist. Brand activism is not limited to famous celebrities. In the digital age of social media, anyone can do it.

Whatever the cause, celebrities have their own reasons for speaking out. Indeed, some celebrities spend a great deal of their time and money organizing in support of a cause. They become more than spokespersons, they are true activists. Their efforts can do much to heighten awareness of their chosen cause, but it also could affect their career. Celebrities should always consider how their support of a particular cause might impact their branding and marketing efforts. Ideally, they should seek to align their activism or philanthropic work with the beliefs and concerns of their target audience.

Cause Marketing and Charity Tie-Ins

It is common for marketing campaigns to use support for charitable causes as a theme. *Cause marketing* is a term I've used to describe this; I also like the term *charity tie-in* when referring to this kind of marketing approach. Sometimes we're told a portion of profits will be donated to a worthy cause or organization. This gives us a good feeling when we buy. When it's a cause that most people can support, such as hunger relief, helping disaster victims, or orphans and widows, who could object? Cause marketing enhances the brand's image, and the donations provide real relief. Consumers get a good feeling knowing their purchase helps to support a worthy cause. Cause marketing can be an effective tool to bring in new customers (or fans), while building brand loyalty. It's a win–win.

Is this always a good idea? When celebrities become activists for political causes, they may also be putting themselves at risk for shunning by fans who oppose their beliefs. There are many glaring examples of this, especially in the entertainment field. The Dixie Chicks (recently rebranded as just "The Chicks"), a superstar country music act, nearly lost their careers when they made a single disparaging comment during a concert in London about then President George W. Bush during the 2003 run-up to the Iraq War. The reaction from their fans and colleagues was swift and severe.

Music and Politics

The demographic for Country music in the United States is largely conservative and republican, and the fans of the Chicks did not take kindly to the stars' comments. There was a widespread spontaneous boycott of their music and they even received death threats. Tours, sponsorships, and record deals were cancelled. It took the act a decade to recover, and they never quite returned to their former level of popularity among Country fans. In 2006, they made a documentary about their experience, called "Shut Up and Sing."

More recently, rapper and TV personality Cardi B lashed out at President Trump during a partial government shutdown. Trump's supporters weren't too pleased with her, yet she probably gained fans. Other celebrities have been fired from TV shows or boycotted by advertisers for expressing unpopular political opinions.

Music is often used in political campaigns. During presidential election cycles in the United States, artists such as (liberal Democrat) Bruce Springsteen have had to formally request that the opposing political party cease using his songs in their rallies. Movie stars such as Adam Sandler and Clint Eastwood have donated large sums of money and even appeared in rallies and conventions for the Republican Party. While many fans don't necessarily care about politics and will still patronize these performers, there are others who will choose not to buy the concert or movie ticket because they oppose the political views of the celebrity in question.

Responsibilities and Risks

We can view the celebrity as an activist from at least two clear perspectives. Both views are valid. An artist might feel the responsibility to use their fame to raise awareness and support for a cause. They care enough to lend their reputation and image to support the cause, even if it risks alienating a portion of their audience. Conversely, and from the perspective of the audience, we go to the concert to be entertained. Why should we care what some musician or sports figure thinks? Some fans would rather not be confronted with an artist's beliefs; they just want to hear the music or watch the game. As in: Shut up and sing. Both of these opposing views are legitimate.

When the cause supported or idea expressed is intensely polarizing, it can become more problematic. Celebrities aren't politicians (in most cases), nor should they behave like politicians. In the case of political causes, it might be wiser from a branding perspective to lend quiet support, perhaps donating money anonymously or appearing at private events in support of the cause. Alternatively, a celebrity might choose to align their views with those of fans, allowing the essence of their brand to more readily resonate with the core of their target audience. Lady Gaga has come out in support of LGBTQ causes, and a sizable portion of her audience consists of individuals who identify as such.

Public support of political causes can dilute brand messaging. It can also engender notoriety for the artist. Extreme political views tend to be controversial by nature. There are times when an artist or company might deliberately choose to stoke controversy in order to raise brand awareness or spur sales (Nike did this successfully recently with former NFL quarterback Colin Kaepernick; Gillette raised the domestic violence issue with their latest "Best a Man Can Be" ad). This can be an effective marketing strategy. Sometimes an organization is willing to take a collective stand on an issue that many care deeply about. Often, they are rewarded.

Causes that are not too polarizing can be more easily incorporated into some brand identities. In the best examples, a synergy is developed between the brand and the cause, enhancing visibility and awareness for both. We see many examples of this today in marketing for all kinds of products. The selected causes and charities tend to be nonpolarizing, usually related to helping the environment, solving hunger and poverty, education, and cures for diseases. (Disaster relief is also a prime candidate for celebrity activism. Think of Willie Nelson and Farm Aid, or George Harrison's legendary Concert for Bangladesh, Bono with AIDS relief in Africa, etc.)

Most people, including celebrities of all types, want to make a positive difference in the world around them. Celebrity brand activism is an effective way for high-visibility individuals to harness the power of their image to resonate with their target audiences in support of a worthy cause. Done right, it can be very powerful. Done poorly, it can cause irreparable harm to the celebrity brand, and doesn't necessarily help the cause. It can be good to decide this earlier rather than later, because you'll attract an audience who either agrees with you—or at least isn't repelled by your views and opinions.

Action Steps:
Take a moment and explore if you would want to become an artist activist.
   1. Do you care passionately about a certain cause?
   2. Do you want to promote that cause through your work somehow?

Doing Well, Doing Good

Celebrity branding and brand activism is a unique opportunity to build brand image for a variety of products and services, including charitable causes. For the reasons cited earlier, brand activism must clearly be approached with caution and be evaluated on a case-by-case basis. There are risks involved. It might be a wise choice for a celebrity not to publicly support causes that tend to polarize or annoy their core demographic. While not for everyone, celebrity brand activism has worked extremely well for some notable people and organizations in promoting their brand.

For musicians starting out in their careers, it may or may not make sense to align themselves with an issue. Speaking out about something one cares deeply about shows a personal side that not every potential fan will be interested to know about. On the other hand, people do respond to authenticity. And of course, if your music overtly addresses some societal issues in its lyrics, attitude, or style, it could make sense to tell the world what you care about. It's possible to attract a sympathetic audience who share your concerns and who will appreciate your willingness to make yourself vulnerable by speaking out. It can make a difference to people in need, and make the world a better place. If they buy your music and come to your shows, all the better. I call it *doing well, while doing good.*

Now that we've looked holistically at some areas to consider early in the business planning process, let's turn to writing your music business plan.

CHAPTER 5

How to Write a Music Business Plan

How to Write a Business Plan for a Musician/Band/ Artist/Music Company

In the last chapter I discussed why and when artists or musicians might choose to write a formal business plan. We considered modes of thinking, social entrepreneurship, and celebrity brand activism in the early stage of planning your business. This chapter details the sections of a business plan and what each section includes. In the following, you'll find a template and method to write your business plan. This format is specifically designed to help anyone starting a music-related business or a band, or launching a career as a music artist. You may want to read through it a few times and follow along with each section's description as you write your own plan.

This chapter will cover these necessary business plan sections:

- Section 1: Cover Page, Name and Logo
- Section 2: Executive Summary
- Section 3: Foundations of the Business
- Section 4: Define Market, Products and Services
- Section 5: Management and Organizational Structure
- Section 6: Marketing and Sales
- Section 7: Financial Information
- Section 8: Conclusion and Sources

When and Why Should You Write a Business Plan?

When should an artist write a business plan? Do you need a business plan for your band? What is in a business plan?

These questions arise frequently when talking to musicians in the early career stage. While the answers may not always be clear cut, it's worthwhile to look at what goes into a business plan, and why you should consider expressing your music business idea using this format. No single answer will apply to everyone, so the best you can do is to look carefully at all the parts and make the decision that seems right for you.

When starting a band, launching yourself as an artist, or embarking on an entrepreneurial journey with an idea for a music company, it should be obvious by now that music is a business and we need to approach it that way. Indeed, this is the overriding message of this entire book. At first, it can feel daunting to consider all that goes into starting a business. When I was young, I resisted learning about business to my detriment. I hope this book helps others not to make that mistake.

We need to face our demons and look them squarely in the eye. No magic bullet exists. No guardian angel will swoop down from the heavens to handle all your business for you. This is a time to be proactive in learning all you can about how business works.

Business Plan Guide: Sections of the Plan

At the outset, you should think of the business plan document as nothing more or less than the expression of your ideas for your music business success and how to achieve your music career goals. That is a good place to start.

You might be focused on selling or licensing your music to businesses (B2B) or to consumers (fans; B2C) or maybe both. Avoid overthinking things early on. You may want to seek investment, partners, or just get organized. Either way, you will start by looking carefully at the market conditions and identifying your prospective customers or fans.

Although templates exist, not every section will apply to a music venture, so I offer one here based on my years of creating my own and teaching others how to do it—for music. As you consider your options, you can find help from an experienced business plan writer. The U.S. Small Business Association website, www.sba.gov, offers a free business plan template. They also have a great program called SCORE which is the acronym for the Service Corps of Retired Executives, www.score.org, where you can be assigned a free mentor to help you write your plan.

When writing your plan, make sure it's easy to scan and can be read easily and quickly. This means using headers, subheaders, and numbered or bulleted points. Avoid large, dense blocks of text, as plan readers don't like to read those. Get some well-written plans to use as a model, and pay attention to your formatting to make your work as accessible as possible.

Use what I share here as a guide to help you write your own plan. Note that the order of creating the sections is usually not the order of presentation. For example, most people write their executive summary last, and it's a good idea to start with the marketing section so you have some ideas about your target market already while you are working on the other sections.

Let's dive right in.

Section 1: Cover Page, Name, and Logo

On the cover page, you should have your business name prominently displayed, along with the logo. You could also include a promotional photograph, especially if you are an artist. The image, logo, colors, and fonts should be carefully selected to create the impression and vibe you want. A metal band's page will probably make a different impression than a classical violinist's. People respond viscerally to images, so think carefully about the image you want to project. Your image identity should resonate with your target audience and your name should stick in their memory.

You should have an additional paragraph (or several short paragraphs) explaining what's behind the name, the significance or special meaning it has, how it influences your business, and what you want it to convey about your products or services to potential customers (or fans). You could also include information about the colors chosen, the logo design, and why you chose the name and images.

Finally, the name should not be in use by anyone else for a similar business concept. It's easy to do a quick search of the Trademark Electronic Search System (TESS), the database maintained by the United States Trademark and Patent Office (USTPO). Also check if anyone is already using the name as an active domain on the Web. If you find no one is using the name you chose, it's a pretty good indication that it is available. Coming up with a good name can be a sticking point for many entrepreneurs, as it seems all the good names are already taken. Your own name may not even be available, if there is another musician with the same name using it.

There are specialists in the advertising industry who get paid a lot of money to think up great names for businesses and products. The name is so important, because it is the one thing you want people to remember about you. One tried and true way of naming is to invent a completely new word. Consider brands such as Xerox, Verizon, Comcast, Kleenex, and Spotify. The ultimate in naming success is when your business or product name becomes synonymous with the product itself. Can you hand me a Kleenex? (Actually it's called a facial tissue, but everyone knows what you meant.) Many artists and actors use pseudonyms. There is a lot riding on your chosen name, so choose it well.

Section 2: Executive Summary

The executive summary is the preview of your product and determines the first impression the reader will get of your business. It is important to write it very clearly and to use professional language. It is your "sales pitch" and is designed to quickly introduce the reader to your business idea and plan. It should be no more than one page in length and cover the following points to sum up for the reader what your business is all about.

Start with the name and location of your business and then describe the mission of the business. Next, describe the products or services you will sell and who your ideal customers are. Include the name and a short bio for each owner of the business, with special emphasis on any aspects of their background that would support your success. Then describe how your business will stand out from the competition. This is called your *differentiation strategy*. Finally, provide a brief overview of the future prospects for your business and for the overall industry. You will revisit most of these topics in later sections of the plan.

It's best to write this part last, after you have written the rest of your plan. Then you can also create your table of contents, which belongs after your cover page and before the executive summary.

Section 3: Foundations of the Business

The foundations section will be a bit longer than the previous sections. Start with a brief description of what your business does, no longer than one or two sentences. This is your *elevator pitch*. Describe the idea as clearly and briefly as possible. Then add a few sentences about the history of the company, your inspiration, and how you came upon the idea. You might mention competitors if they gave you the idea or talk about the moment you realized your business idea could succeed. Try to write in a way that is clear and compelling, to actively engage your reader.

Share the long-term *vision* for your company and then include your formal *mission statement*. The vision should include not only where you are now, but what you see as the future of your company, maybe in five years from now. The mission statement describes what your company does, why you do it, how you get it done, and who you do it for. Use descriptive terminology that projects the image for your company in a way you feel proud of.

At this point, lay out the specific objectives for the business: what exactly you will provide, change, create, fix, or improve for your customers. Explain the important reasons why your customers will choose you, your product, or your service. What will customers get from your company? Write about some specific financial goals you will achieve with the business in the first years, and how you will achieve those goals.

Describe the revenue you will earn from selling your products on a weekly, monthly, and annual basis, how many of each you will sell at what price, and to how many customers. This is just a rough summary; you will give more details in the financial section of your plan which comes later. You might want to include a chart or graph here to illustrate your goals.

Next, briefly discuss the key leadership roles and how the business is organized. You will write about this in more detail later, but for now describe the form of business ownership (partnership, sole proprietor, LLC, nonprofit, corporation) and why this form makes the most sense regarding the tax and liability issues your business will face. You should also mention the key skills the founders bring to the organization, including yourself.

This might be a good place to mention any plans you have for social entrepreneurship, how you will give back to the community, improve people's lives, volunteer time or money to charitable causes, or show respect to your neighbors and community. Mention the values that your business will hold dear.

Section 4: Define Market, Products and Services

This part of the plan should be more lengthy, as you must describe not only your products and services in detail, but also why they are competitive within your general and target markets.

Start by describing the specific market your business will be in. Do research by reading articles, visiting websites and blogs, talking to others in the industry, and observing other businesses and their customers. Make sure you have a good understanding of your corner of the industry before writing your description. Consider the current state of the overall music industry and future trends. Take geographical location into account, as well as local regulations or laws that impact the market.

Do the best you can to describe the demand for your product or service in the market and the niche you will initially target. Include some details about the demographics of your prospects, such as age, location, lifestyle, income, education, and ethnicity. Also include their psychographics: what they care about, what motivates their behavior, and why they will want your product. Use some footnotes in this section to show where you got your information and lend extra credibility to your claims. Citing reliable sources will lend authority and boost believability to skeptical plan readers in your statements about the future. With your sources, quality is more important than quantity. Don't use Wikipedia as a cited source as it is publicly sourced and not regarded as authoritative.

Describe your top selling products and services, how much you sell them for (unit cost) and how you deliver them to the customer. If you are giving concerts, for example, you can describe the experience for the fans, ticket price, how many tickets you will sell at each show, and how many shows you will do weekly, monthly, or annually. Compare your product or service to your main competitors. Be specific, using the competitors' names, and write about what you will do better than them. You could also do a full SWOT analysis, analyzing both your business and your competitors' strengths, weaknesses, opportunities, and threats (more on the SWOT later in this chapter).

Section 5: Management and Organizational Structure

Although you may have previously mentioned any partners in the executive summary, include more information on how the business will be organized in this section (Figure 5.1). This can include key players in the organization, the experience and skills they will bring to your operation, and the responsibilities for each role. If you don't know their names yet, use job titles and qualifications for the role.

Action Steps:

1. List the organization's key players and the experience and skills they'll bring to your organization.
2. If you wish, describe the responsibilities for each role.
3. Draw an organization chart, if needed.

Write about your leadership philosophy and why it is a good fit for the kind of business you are in. Discuss your management and employment policies, whether you will use outside vendors, compensation for employees, benefits offered such as health insurance or retirement fund, your legal and accounting needs, transportation, purchasing, and critical business systems or software you will use.

Even though you might be starting with only yourself, try to imagine what your company might look like as it grows. Some famous artists have large teams to work with them on tours, marketing, writing, producing, or on other aspects of their business. These people must be organized into teams. The way you organize your business is crucial to future success.

Action Steps:

1. Outline your vision for future growth of the business.
2. Describe where you want to be in three years and in five years.
3. Make sure you mention the form of the business, whether an LLC, type of corporation, or a nonprofit, and why you chose that form.
4. Clarify how the chosen business entity will affect your taxes, your culture, and your ability to succeed.
5. Mention customer service policies or employment manuals.
6. Describe your logistics, such as where you will be based, any facilities or equipment needs, storage, and communications. You might want

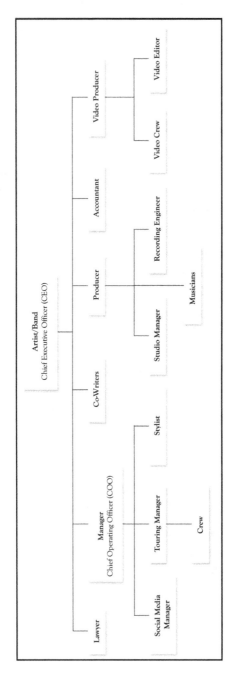

Figure 5.1 Organizational structure for the artist-entrepreneur

to showcase a facility or specialized gear, to prove that you are ready to compete in your market.

Section 6: Marketing and Sales

The ultimate goal of marketing is sales. In this section, you will clarify your methods and strategies to access your market and get sales. In Section 4 you described your market, your expertise in understanding your target niche and demographic, and how you will market to them. You need sales to have revenue (income), and you need revenue to have a business. To connect with your target market, you will need cost-effective channels to reach them.

It's now time to get specific about your marketing mix.

Action Steps:

1. If you plan to use social media, name the platforms and specific strategies, along with how much time you need for each.
2. If you will attend trade conferences, name those, too.
3. You might consider other types of marketing or advertising, such as direct mail, sponsorships, paid ads, free samples, contests, posters and flyers, and word of mouth.
4. Describe all of your marketing strategies, and how each one will support your business and help you meet your goals.
5. Consider how your competitors market themselves, what they do well, or how they could improve.
6. Explain specifically why your customers will choose you over the competition.

Describe your sales strategy, paying attention to your pricing and sales channels. Will you partner with affiliates for distribution, or have you found some unique way to get your product or service to the end user? Describe the value proposition for your customers (why they will buy) and also your unique selling points (USPs). Describe your plans for marketing and sales in a holistic way, and discuss how various players in the company will contribute. You can mention how much time and effort will be allocated to marketing and sales compared to all the other things your company must do.

Section 7: Financial Information

Artist-entrepreneurs often struggle with this part. You are asked to make a realistic assessment of the future. Of course, no one can see the future, but you can certainly make some believable projections. First, talk about what it will cost to start and run your business (startup costs) for at least the first year. Be as realistic as possible and base your projections in solid research. If you need certain equipment or facilities, you can research what those costs are; the same is true for other startup costs, such as your marketing and production.

Action Steps:
1. Mention how you will acquire the needed funds for startup and be specific about what the funds are for. A good way to organize the information is to create a spreadsheet in Excel or Google Docs. Some costs might be one-time outlays while others may be supplies you need on an ongoing basis, your rent, or other recurring expenses.
2. Create an income statement to show your first year expenses, month by month. You should also show any revenues if you will have them. When you put it all together it should give the reader a clear view of your first year financial picture. While many businesses don't earn money in the first year, some do. Your income and expenses projection should also take into account any taxes you will owe.

After projecting your first year month by month, the next step is to show years two and three by quarters (every three months). Some startups try to project further out, but it really isn't needed since so much can change in a few years. Your main goal with the financials is to get as accurate a picture as possible of your first few years in business.

There's an art to creating these kinds of projections. You should be positive but realistic, and avoid any outlandish claims. It's okay to aim a bit high in your projections, but be careful that you don't make them based only on hope. Do the research so you can back up your financial projections. Don't forget to include footnotes to your references and sources for the financial projections.

Section 8: *Conclusion and Sources*

In this final section you should thank the reader for reading your plan and stress your preparedness and enthusiasm for succeeding with your business. Make it clear that you are available to answer any questions they might have and include your contact information again. On the very last page, include your footnotes and organize your sources alphabetically in a bibliography using the Modern Language Association (MLA) style. It's a good idea to have a dozen or more sources in your bibliography to lend credibility to your plan and show readers that you've done your research.

As you consider whether or not you should write a business plan, or if you have decided you want to write one, you will need to study up on all the areas I have written about here. My brief guide here shows how to put a plan together, and you will need to do some homework before you can write each section.

I recommend you do not assume your reader knows anything. Many new business plan writers make the mistake of being too vague, or not including enough specifics. This awakens suspicion in the mind of the reader, as they begin to wonder what else you aren't telling them. In some cases, less is more. However, with the business plan, more information can be helpful to your reader. The goal is to try to answer every question your reader might have before they can ask it. Be extremely thorough, but be careful not to go overboard with unnecessary information.

Writing a business plan helps you learn important things about yourself and your music.

Action Steps:
Answer these questions to help you form your plan.
1. What motivates you to want to be in music?
2. What are the things you are good at?
3. What are the things you need help with?
4. Where do you want to be in three, in five, or in ten years?
5. What are your likes and dislikes?
6. What resources do you have, or can you get?
7. Do you need investors or partners to start your business?
8. How will you stay in control of your business and career?
9. What is the market for your music?

These questions, and others, will help you create your business plan, which can be an exercise in deep personal learning.

The Pitch Deck

The irony is that many potentially interested parties initially won't take the time to read your plan. This means the entrepreneurial business plan writer will also need to create a *pitch deck* to get the key points in the plan across quickly. (This is sometimes called a *sales deck* or *investor deck*.) If you've ever watched the show "Shark Tank," you've seen how the business owner is expected to very quickly pitch their idea, using slides and images. You might have only five minutes to pitch, so be ready!

Having a pitch deck to show potential partners is smart, whether they are musicians, labels, booking agents, investors, publicists, venue managers, or tour operators. They will be more likely to quickly understand your business idea this way. If your materials are well written and you can present them effectively, you'll be seen as being ultra-prepared and ready for success.

According to PayPal cofounder and serial entrepreneur Peter Thiel, a pitch deck should include the following slides:

1. Problem
2. Solution
3. Market size
4. Product
5. Traction
6. Team
7. Competition
8. Financials
9. Amount being raised

Ultimately, a well-written business plan will help you to define your business, understand the market, define your product, outline your strategy, and create an operating plan. Additionally, your plan will help you figure out how to find and manage the people you will need, fulfill your administrative needs, and project financial results that make clear how the business should perform. Your plan will clearly outline any potential obstacles to success, and explain your strategies to get around them.

Now that you have the components of your business plan, let's dig a bit deeper into the marketing aspect and learn what goes into a marketing proposal.

General Market Description and the Marketing Proposal

With a music business plan, the sections on marketing and sales are usually the most challenging parts to write. They are also among the most important. Now we'll take a closer look at defining your market and learn how to create a marketing proposal.

Many music business neophytes freeze like a deer in the headlights when asked to create a marketing proposal. Let's demystify some of the hype. Recall that the business plan helps you discover and learn about your future success in music. This doesn't have to be a dry exercise. A marketing proposal is a marketing plan. To start, write a description of your market. I'll take you through the following steps.

Action Steps:
Clarify your market.
1. Describe the size and location of your market.
2. Age?
3. Geographic location?
4. Hobbies?
5. Favorable trends related to them.

Next, go a little deeper.

1. Thinking about those people who will listen to your music, pay you to record or perform, attend your concerts, or buy your merchandise, how do they "use" your music?
2. Do they listen in order to relax, to party, for dancing, or for some other reason?
3. Could your music be used in films, video games, sporting events, or advertising?
4. Do you sell your music primarily to other businesses (B2B) or directly to the consumer (B2C)? What are the main purposes of your music, why does it exist?

5. Put yourself in the shoes of your ideal listener and imagine how they will use your music on a daily basis.

Action Steps:
1. Write about your music business concept, including all your ideas, and then describe how people will consume the music you create.
2. Write down the names of others who create closely similar products or services, and how and where those concepts are used.

We will get more specific later with comparing your idea to some direct competitors, but for now, make sure to write down everything you can think of about your music business idea, plus how and why it should succeed. Next, you'll extrapolate from the target demographic to identify a larger sample size to figure out who your future fans are.

Defining Your Market

Now that you've zoomed in to look carefully at your prospects, you can draw from that to get a better idea of the total market you are aiming for. For example, if you believe that you would be popular with college students, you can research the number of colleges around the country, how many students attend college, and where they are concentrated.

Market location: If you tend to go over well with college crowds in Massachusetts, you could assume you'll also do well at colleges in Chicago, Ann Arbor, or New Orleans.

Market size: Come up with a realistic estimate of the size of your market and where you will find your biggest fans. This kind of metric will help guide you in your marketing efforts. The following steps in the process will lead you to create your marketing proposal.

Describing Your Products and Services

Next, we can talk about what you're selling.

1. Are you primarily a live act who can survive and thrive from selling concert tickets?
2. Do you get revenues from streaming, licensing, or sales of downloads or ring tones?
3. Will you write songs to be recorded by other artists?
4. Do you sell merchandise?
5. Do you teach students or offer educational workshops?

List your top three money-making products or services. Estimate how much money you expect to earn from each.

1. What is the unit cost? For example, how many tickets can you sell per show, and at what price for each ticket?
2. How many shows can you do per week, month, or year?
3. What kind of merchandise are you selling? T-shirts and hats?
4. How many will you sell and at what price each?

How much profit can you earn from each sale?

1. Will you have your music licensed for use in visual media like films, advertising, or video games?
2. Do you make recordings for a flat rate?

There are many ways to earn money in the music industry, so think about all the ways you will earn money and write them all down as precisely as you can. It's okay to be ambitious here, but you should also consider carefully what might be realistic, given your target market size and the competition. Sometimes you will need to make an educated guess. As with your business plan, you should cite some reliable sources if you can find them.

Fulfillment Channels

Now that we know something about our market and the products or services we will sell, we must consider how we'll make the sales and deliver our product. Think of every possible way someone could purchase your music. How will you make sure people get access to your product when they want it? Think of all that could go wrong, from technical glitches to severe weather or storms that would keep you from getting to the concert venue. You should have contingency plans for everything with the goal of never disappointing your fans.

Also, consider your pay systems, how you will get paid, and how you will manage your money as it comes in and goes out to pay for the things you will need in order to produce and deliver your product. If you have to pay people, whether for products or services, how will you accomplish that? Will you have a paywall on your website or use a third party payments company to accept credit cards? Can you accept cash? Being in business means you'll always deliver for your customers and you'll always get paid. It's important to understand the supply chain and have a fulfillment (sales and delivery) plan that will work.

Competitive Analysis and Comparisons

Take a closer look at your competition. As mentioned earlier, music is part of the entertainment industry, so competition could come from other entertainment market sectors like movies, video games, or sports. People have limited disposable income (the money they have left after they pay for everything they must pay for, like rent, utilities, and food); this means you are technically competing with anything else they could spend their money on in the entertainment sector. Your competitors might also come from other sectors, like vacations, spas, restaurants, or apparel industries.

For our purposes, consider those making and selling similar products and services as direct competitors. If you are a band, what other bands are most like you? If you are a session musician, who are some other successful players of your instrument?

Action Steps:
1. Pick at least two or three direct competitors and analyze their marketing, branding, and products or services.
2. Write a short paragraph about each competitor.

3. Describe what they do particularly well, and what you think they could do better. Then describe how you will set yourself apart from them, and why customers would choose you instead.

4. Consider how you can improve on what they do for their fans and how you will communicate that to your prospective audience?

SWOT Your Business

SWOT is an acronym for *Strengths, Weaknesses, Opportunities, and Threats* faced by your business. It is also part of any business plan, and you should include it with your marketing proposal. Strengths and weaknesses are about your internal aspects while opportunities and threats refer to external factors.

For strengths and weaknesses, think about this from the perspective of your customers or fans. What is it about you, your product, or your service that they will find compelling? What will they perceive as unique or different? Any advantage you have is a strength. Your weaknesses might have to do with difficulties in creating or delivering your product, high costs for production, or problems with getting your product out. Write about how you might leverage your strengths and overcome any weaknesses.

Opportunities will come from the marketplace, for example, if there is a strong demand for what you do. Generally, opportunities result in revenues for your business (earning money). The threats could be from competitors with strong name recognition or better advertising budget and draw. There are barriers to entry for every market. Brainstorm ways to overcome the hurdles you'll inevitably face when breaking into the market, as well as how to capitalize on any positive trends.

The Marketing Proposal

If you've been writing down the answers to all these questions as I've outlined them, you will be well on your way to having a solid marketing proposal. A good proposal will take all the careful thought and research you've been doing and distill it into a written plan for the coming year. There isn't one way to write this, so you can feel free to create your plan using elements that make the most sense for your own business situation. Following are some possible ideas about structure, and how you can pull it all together in your proposal.

First, write a brief marketing plan executive summary to introduce the products or services you offer and to summarize what will be in the marketing proposal. This is helpful to anyone who might read it, such as A&Rs, managers, label partners, producers, investors, or colleagues, and will provide a quick overview of what's in the proposal.

Next, give a brief description of your target market, including relevant demographics, and mention why they might prefer your product over your competitors'. Use numbered or bulleted points to make this simple and clear.

The next section will be about your specific goals. Keep this section short, and be sure to use the SMART goals acronym: Specific, Measurable, Attainable, Relevant, and Timely. For example:

> We will play 200 shows next year in the mainland United States with average attendance of 200 ticket buyers per show at $20.00 per ticket. This will increase our listener base as reflected by a 30 percent increase in monthly streams on Spotify by the end of the year.

Now, write down your marketing strategy, keeping in mind your USP, or what makes you different or unique. You should explain exactly how you intend to achieve your goals. Be as specific as you can about how you intend to reach your prospects with your marketing efforts.

Finally, write your budget if you have one, outlining how much you will spend and on what.

It's a good idea to revisit and update your marketing plan at least once a year. You will need to evaluate what's working and what isn't. Be objective and honest in your assessment, and make changes as needed to adapt to changes in your market and your business. Above all, be creative in your efforts.

Now, you know how to research your market, how to brainstorm about marketing strategies, write your music business plan, and what goes into a marketing proposal. Use this information as a springboard to learn more about how to promote your music, develop a fan base, and reach your prospective audience. We will return to more marketing topics later in the book. First, let's have a look at how to form your business entity.

CHAPTER 6

Create Your Business Entity

When I was in college, I performed at a jazz festival with my quartet. They paid me by check. When I visited my local bank to deposit the check, I ran into a problem. This wasn't good, because I needed to pay the other musicians from this check. At the teller window, I learned the bank couldn't deposit the check into my account. I asked why. The conversation went like this:

Bank Teller: It isn't made out to you.

Me: But it is made out to the Tom Stein Quartet, and I'm Tom Stein.

Bank Teller: But you aren't the Tom Stein Quartet.

Me: I see. What should I do?

Bank Teller: You have two options. You can go back to whoever wrote the check and ask them to write out another check to you, or you can open a business banking account with us and deposit the check to that account.

I liked the sound of that second idea, so I sat down with their business banking officer to open an account. I learned that to open a business account I would need to get a business certificate, also called a d.b.a. (stands for "doing business as"), which I would need to fill out and then file with the local clerk of the county court. This experience was my initial introduction to business entity formation. Ironically, years later I ended up teaching students how to set up their music business entities in my college courses. To anyone with a business or legal background, this information would not be new, but I've found most musicians share some confusion on the legal aspects of setting up and running a music business, such as a band. Following are some pointers and what you really need to know.

Since I'm not a lawyer or an accountant, I need to provide a disclaimer that I am not legally allowed to dispense legal or financial advice, and that you should always consult your own attorney and accountant for advice on specific situations, such as the best way to form the legal entity of your business.

Sole Proprietor: Should You Register?

If I cut my neighbor's grass or paint her house, and she pays me, I'm in business. Technically I would be called a *sole proprietor*. This is exactly what it sounds like: I am in business for myself, by myself, as the owner of my business. I can hire others to help me, but it won't change the fact that it's my business. There is no further paperwork necessary. As I explained above, there are some reasons why you might consider registering your name as a sole proprietor using the d.b.a. form. For example, if you operate your business and accept payments under a name other than your birth name, or wish to protect your own name from being used by others, you will need to file a d.b.a.

It takes time and hard work to build and protect your reputation. A good reputation is extremely valuable as others consider it when deciding whether or not to work with you. Imagine if someone else starts doing business under the same name as you, and does inferior work. Your reputation will suffer, and you could lose business. Registering your name as a d.b.a. with the clerk of the local court system protects the use of your name from infringement of this kind. If someone else starts using your name in a similar type of business, you can legally make them stop. The court would back you, as long as you can prove you were there first. Registering your name as a d.b.a. is the best way to get that proof.

The court will protect you from infringement, because they wish to protect the public from confusion. This means that even if someone started using a name that was not identical, but similar to yours, you could probably stop them.

The Corporate Veil

Another reason you might decide to formalize your business's name and business structure is to protect from legal liability. There's an additional step involved. Making the best choice of entity for protection from legal liability might depend on where you live and your budget. It could also depend on the type of activities you engage in. I probably don't need to form a corporation to mow my neighbor's lawn, but if I am mowing lawns all day, every day, I might need to consider liability protection.

To protect your personal assets and future income from business liability, you could buy liability insurance, sometimes called a *bond*. Or you might create a business entity for the express purpose of separating your personal assets (such as your home, car, instruments, and savings) from your business assets. Remember that litigants can make a claim on future earnings, so even if you don't have any assets now, you'll still need some kind of liability protection.

Let's imagine everything that could go wrong. We live in a litigious society, where people decide to sue at the drop of a hat. A client might sue you if musicians showed up late to their wedding dinner, claiming that you ruined their special day. They might seek monetary damages from you. A musician or audience member might trip on one of your speaker cables and break their arm, suing you for medical expenses plus pain and suffering. Especially when you are successful, you are more likely to be a target of a frivolous lawsuit, because people see an opportunity to get money out of you by convincing a judge that you were liable for some perceived harm to them. This stuff happens, and it's a part of doing business everywhere. Enter: the corporate veil.

A corporation is a business structure that separates your personal assets from your business. This means, should you be sued and lose, the claimant cannot attach your personal possessions to the judgment. They will be limited to taking what is in the business. This means you can never lose more than you've invested in the business, except maybe your good name and reputation you worked so hard to build. Every business owner needs some kind of strategy to protect them from liability. Let's quickly examine a few of the more common business structures used for liability protection.

Limited Liability Companies and Partnerships (LLC, LLP)

We've already described what a sole proprietor is. For many businesses, the next logical step would be to form a *Limited Liability Company* (LLC) or a *Limited Liability Partnership* (LLP). Contrary to what some people might think, these business structures are not corporations. They are companies, either owned by a single individual (LLC) or by a partnership with multiple owners (LLP). Each of these business forms do exactly what the name implies: protect the owners from liability. They are chartered at the state level, so the annual fee to maintain them varies from state to state. In Massachusetts, where I live, the annual fee is $500.00 for an LLC.

One advantage of the LLC is that your income is only taxed at the personal level, and you can file your taxes for the company on the same return as your personal taxes, both state and federal. If you have a partnership, you must file an additional tax document, called a K-1 (IRS Form 1065), for your company's earnings, but the taxes are still paid by the individuals on their personal returns. For this reason, the LLC, LLP, and some other corporate structures (we will discuss next) are sometimes called *flow-through entities*. As with any decisions that will impact the legal status of your business and finances, it is important to consult with a qualified attorney and also an accountant when choosing your business entity. They can advise you on how to choose the best form, based on your personal situation, and your financial, legal, and business needs.

Corporate Business Entities: C-Corp, S-Corp, and Nonprofit

Depending on the nature and size of your business, you may feel you need a more robust structure to manage your business and finances. For most companies, a *C-Corporation* (C-Corp) or an *S-Corporation* (S-Corp) will be the logical next step. Both types of corporations also protect from liability but do quite a bit more.

As with anything, there are advantages and disadvantages. According to the Fundera website:

> S-Corps are considered "pass-through" entities, where the business's profits and losses are reported on the business owner's income.

C-Corps are taxed both at the corporate level, and on the owners' personal income tax returns, if corporate income is distributed to the corporation's shareholders as dividends.

Also according to Fundera, the C-Corp is a better choice if one wishes to raise venture capital (investments), issue shares of stock, pay out profits to shareholders as dividends, or have foreign (non-United States) stockholders. These things are harder to do with the S-Corp (e.g., shareholders must be U.S. citizens), while the main benefit of the S-Corp is that owners pay income tax on their profits only. With the C-Corp, income is taxed at both the corporate level and on the personal income tax. Therefore, with the C-Corp there is *double taxation*. There are definitely some trade-offs here.

Another possibility is to set up a *nonprofit*, sometimes also called a *not-for-profit*, or a 501(c)(3) under the U.S. tax code. Nonprofit organizations have the benefit of protecting most revenues from taxation, but they also have some strings attached. For example, nonprofits must have a board of directors that is required to ensure the company stays focused on the purpose it was set up for, usually to solve some pressing problem or cater to a specific need in society. Nonprofits must also show that they are providing in-kind services to the municipality where they are located, so that they add value to the community in lieu of paying property taxes. Many religious organizations, schools, medical providers, and social services businesses are set up as nonprofits.

Organizing as a nonprofit doesn't mean the business can't make a profit. They are allowed to earn profits, so long as those profits are devoted to their unique cause in some way, and not the primary reason for their activities. It's understood that nonprofits must answer to a higher cause, unlike other corporate entities where the profit motive is usually paramount. Nonprofits pay their employees and officers, but they aren't supposed to pay exceedingly high salaries. There have been controversies around this convention, which is subject to interpretation. There are some officers of large nonprofits, such as the Red Cross, who have been in the news due to earning high six-figure salaries. Another point for consideration with nonprofits is that their financial records are made available to the public on request. This is not the case with privately held for-profit entities.

Organizational Structure

Now, we can dig a bit deeper into the internal organization of your company starting with leadership. Along with questions about employees, partners, business structure, compensation, policies, taxes, costs, and business processes, we should consider your leadership philosophy.

Leadership Philosophy

At the outset of writing this book I decided I wanted to draw from areas of business outside of the music and entertainment industries. The way you will lead is a crucial aspect of building and running any business. Leaders at the top set the tone, and there are as many approaches and ways of thinking about leadership as there are leaders.

One of my favorite writers on this subject is Ray Dalio, the billionaire hedge-fund manager who advocates radical transparency in leadership. Others, such as the late MIT professor and corporate consultant Peter Drucker, have written numerous books on corporate leadership and philosophy of management. There is a large body of academic research into organizational behavior and leadership. Since this is a book about management for musicians, I've done my own research into leadership philosophies in the music industry. How leaders lead effectively is a fascinating subject for investigation.

Most management issues and challenges will be recognizable to anyone working in a large organization. Leaders and employees typically complain of being stuck in endless meetings that keep them from getting into the "zone" where they can be productive. According to Drucker, who conducted ingenious research over many decades into how organizations are managed: "The level of productivity in an organization is inversely proportional to the number of meetings held." This is one of my all-time favorite quotes.

Is this how you want your company to function? There are many other traps set for the novice manager, such as how to motivate employees, how to be fair, how to make good decisions, and how to best reward and honor employees appropriately for their contributions. The 20th century psychologist Abraham Maslow developed elegant theories on the hierarchies of human needs, which apply to organizational leadership and

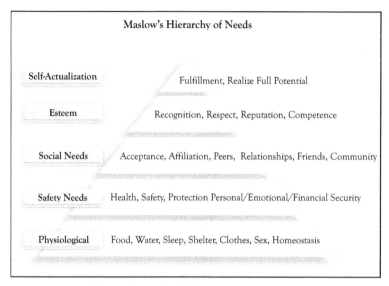

Figure 6.1 Maslow's hierarchy of human needs

philosophy as well (Figure 6.1). Most leaders struggle mightily in hiring the right people for their organizations, and keeping them motivated to do great work.

There is a difference between owning a business and being self-employed. A business owner can walk away from the business, and it will continue to earn money; self-employed people stop getting paid when they stop working. I'm not making a value judgment here; it's fine to be either one, but it's best to be honest with yourself about what you are trying to achieve. Some businesses can be replicated or franchised, in order to achieve scale. Not every business is meant to work this way. As we discuss philosophies of leadership in organizations, let's now turn to a model of how things might work. This model grew out of concepts I've culled from my research and from my direct experiences working and leading in businesses.

Action Steps:

You will want to ask yourself a number of questions. The following list is not all inclusive, but can be used as a starting point in thinking about how you want your business to function. It's best to consider these questions while thinking about the business entity formation as well.

Consider and answer these questions.

- Will you be the owner of your company or will there be multiple owners? If more than one, how many owners will your business have?
- What will the roles and responsibilities be of any partners in the business?
- What form or structure makes the most sense for your company regarding possible tax liability?
- Have you considered the costs involved with setting up and running your chosen business structure?
- What will the paperwork be like for your chosen business structure? Will it be manageable?
- Will you have employees? If so, how many? Will you consider letting them become partners in the business later on?
- How will decisions get made? Will you be the main decision maker at your company?
- How will you protect your personal assets from liability?

Vision, Mission, and Strategic Imperatives

It all starts with the *vision*. The founder or head of the company is primarily responsible for formulating and broadcasting the vision to everyone inside and outside of the company. This is the primary role of the leader. This doesn't mean they must create the vision alone. They can and should solicit input from their team, their employees, and their customers. This could be accomplished using surveys, focus groups, meetings, and conversations with all stakeholders about what they believe the core vision of the company should be. It can take time to come up with a coherent vision which resonates with everyone. Gathering opinions and ideas from employees also elicits buy-in from those tasked with doing the work. Employees are usually happier when they have a clear understanding of the company vision and have some say in determining how the work is to be accomplished.

Craft your *vision statement* of no more than one to two sentences. The vision statement should describe in clear language why the organization exists. For an artist or band, it might read something like this:

The (name of band or artist) provides listeners with music they can enjoy and relate to as they go about their lives. This music is accessible and fun, and makes the world a happier place for those who listen.

Action Step:
Create your own vision statement.
Try filling in the blanks to start.

> [NAME OF BUSINESS] offers [WHAT YOU OFFER] to [YOUR TARGET MARKET], so they can [WHAT THEY GET]. The [WHAT YOU OFFER] is [UNIQUE DESCRIPTION] and helps/makes/achieves [OUTCOME OF WHAT YOU OFFER].

Importantly, the vision must motivate the employees or partners to engage in your business by working hard over time to fulfill its promise. This means it must align with their own reasons for wanting to be part of your company. Casting the vision so that others will align with it is the most important job of the founder or CEO. The vision is what keeps people coming to work every day and caring about the success of the business. It's more important than the paycheck. After all, they can earn a paycheck pretty much anywhere.

The next step is to craft a solid *mission statement*. The mission statement lays out exactly what the business must do, to support the vision. A mission statement should consist of one or two brief paragraphs, and might read like this:

The mission of (name of band or artist) is to produce and release creative recordings of original music that are uplifting and of the highest possible quality in terms of production value. The same music will also be performed in live shows and concerts at small, medium, and large music venues around the world. The unique concert experience and highest quality recordings are a top priority, and will fulfill a need for diverse audiences to unwind, relax, enjoy life, and have a great time.

Additionally, music produced by (name of band or artist) will be licensed to appear in movies, television shows, video games, advertising, and other visual media and at special events. Taken altogether, the music of (name of band or artist) will be known the world over as a result of being easily discoverable on streaming platforms and through other diverse channels. A top-notch marketing team will be in place to drive audiences to discovering and enjoying the music of (name of band or artist).

Reading this mission statement, we get a clear idea of what must occur for the vision to be achieved. Everything in the mission statement flows directly from the vision; it's clear exactly WHAT (mission) must happen in order for the WHY (vision) to come to fruition.

Action Step:
Using the preceding example, craft your own mission statement.

Remember, we are talking about the future. This means that the vision and mission statements are aspirational. Together, they paint a picture of where the organization is going, and what it hopes to become. (This doesn't mean the language is aspirational—avoid using the word "try.") The vision and mission statements are living, breathing things and should be updated from time to time as the organization grows and changes in response to external conditions in the market and to internal priorities.

In the third step, we define our *strategic imperatives.* This is the fun part, because the leader has an opportunity to learn from some smart people. The strategic imperatives are where the rubber meets the road; this is about HOW the mission will be accomplished, in order to realize the vision. We already know what we must do, and why. Now it's time to figure out how to best do it.

Eliciting input from those tasked with carrying out the work is best achieved by first "getting the right people on the bus," as described by corporate strategist and Stanford professor Jim Collins in his legendary best-selling book *Good to Great* (Harper Business, 2001). Hiring the right people is more than half the battle. They can show you how best to achieve the mission, and fulfill the vision of your business.

Action Step:
Define your own strategic imperatives.

Employees: Hiring, Motivation, and Culture

Not every organization has employees. Some hire outside vendors (outsourcing), and some have partners and associates. For now, as we consider how to attract the right people to an organization, pay attention to the recruitment and interview process. Many job interviews go off the rails because the interviewers are incompetent and ask irrelevant questions. The proper way to conduct an interview is as follows:

1. Explain the vision and mission of the organization clearly.
2. Ask the potential partner how they would work to achieve the mission in the job they are applying to. (This might include them telling you some stories about how they did similar things in the past.)
3. Listen and take notes about the answers.

Of course, this is a bit simplified, and it is necessary to first determine whether or not the person is prepared and has the right skills for the job. Since you can't interview every applicant, use a rubric to carefully screen the applicants using their resume, cover letter, and supporting application materials. As an example, if you are looking for a support musician for your band, you should first audition them and see how they play. Then, you can talk about the vision and mission, if you think they play well enough. Whoever you decide to work with ought to be able to explain or show you what they will do (strategic imperatives) to achieve your shared goals (the mission) that ultimately supports the success of the business (the vision).

This model of vision, mission, and strategic imperative is taught to students in business school, where they work together on case studies to analyze real-world examples of successful or failed companies. A better way to learn is to apply models like this one to your own venture in the music business and to examine and compare the models used by other successful businesses, companies, and artists. A little research and digging on websites should make clear how they model their business and give you more useful ideas about creating your own models.

Stakeholder Alignment

I've previously used the word *stakeholder* to refer to anyone inside or outside a company that is impacted in some way by the business. This includes employees, owners, managers, vendors, partners, stockholders (if there are company shares), and of course, the customers. *Culture* is an oft-used buzzword in the world of organizational behavior. One factor that influences the culture in an organization is how well all stakeholders are aligned with the vision and mission, and for those that work in the business, how the structure of their work is determined. The culture of an organization might seem fixed, but can change over time, and is also a function of leadership style.

Some company cultures are transparent and inclusive, with management always looking to hear constructive criticism and input from employees and customers in order to improve processes, products, and services. I call this a *bottom-up* organizational culture, since information flows from the lower ranks up to senior leaders. Other cultures might be considered *top-down*, where top leaders dictate to managers and employees what will happen in a hierarchical way. Information flows from the top down to the lower ranks.

Leaders seeking to elicit buy-in from employees will allow them a say in the design of their work. After all, the frontline employees have the best grasp of what the customers want and can spot the friction points. They might know how to solve the problems. Having an open, bottom-up managerial style and culture might be beneficial in this case. In the army, where the generals have a wide view of things, a top-down structure might work best, especially during a battle where someone with a view from the top is needed to give orders, with lives at stake. Ultimately, it's the job of the leader to get all stakeholders in alignment with the mission and vision, whether using a top-down or bottom-up style.

The Organizational Chart

Think about your future company. Whether you're a band, record label, booking agency, production house, or a solo artist, or any other type of business, you never really go it alone. The DIY (Do It Yourself) ethos is actually DIWO (Do It With Others), as we will discover in the next chapter. If you are a sole proprietor with no employees, you may have to hire other freelancers to complete tasks you lack the skills or time to do yourself. Just as you have contracts with your business clients, you will need to negotiate and execute formal contracts with those you hire and rely on to deliver your products or services to the customers and fans. As you work with collaborators, partners, employees, or vendors, you will need some kind of structure for these relationships.

In Chapter 5 we discussed the organizational structure of the business plan. Let's return for a moment to the organizational chart. An organizational chart is a model for how people relate to each other in a hierarchy. There're many ways to go about creating one. For the aforementioned scenario, it is pretty simple. You are at the top, and all others report directly to you.

If you have employees, managers, and vendors, the chart could become a bit more involved. For example, the primary managers report directly to you, and the employees or vendors will report to the managers. There can also be dual reports, for example, the director of marketing reports to you and also to the director of sales. Product development might also report to marketing and sales. And so on.

There are some organizations which have a flat structure, where everyone works as a coequal team member. A band might work that way, but when there is a disagreement among the members, who makes the final decision? Democracy doesn't always work so well in a band situation. Best to have hierarchies mapped out in advance, so that the team doesn't splinter and become fragmented in the face of difficult choices.

With a nonprofit, the president or CEO reports to the board of directors. Some startup businesses have an informal board of advisors. The larger an organization gets, the harder it is to design an organizational structure to streamline operations and support the business's growth. The organizational chart doesn't need to be complicated, but it does need to work. Survey how other similar businesses are organized, and think carefully about the best structure for your business. There isn't one right way of doing things, but it's important to align all stakeholders with the vision and mission. The structure of the company needs to facilitate this.

The choice of organizational structure affects the culture of the business. A top-down hierarchical style of governance could lead to a toxic work culture. Organizations that choose a more transparent and inclusive style of management tend to be rated more highly by employees and customers. Virgin Atlantic CEO Richard Branson has said that the customer does not always come first; the employee comes first. According to him, an employee or partner who feels valued and well treated is more likely to treat the customer well. Branson believes in treating employees well enough so they will not want to leave the organization. Virgin has a low turnover rate, is rated highly for employee satisfaction, and is a profitable company. I'm also a big fan of Chobani Yogurt founder and CEO Hamdi Ulukaya's "Anti-CEO Playbook." Hamdi stresses that companies need to consider how they can meet the needs of their communities rather than the other way around.

As a leader primarily responsible for crafting the vision and mission, communicating that information to others, and executing on strategy, your organizational chart should facilitate achieving the company's goals. An organizational chart is also part of the business plan, as we discussed in the previous chapter. The chart should be created at initial stage, and then be adjusted to fit the business as it grows and matures. Many corporate CEOs hire consultants to help them figure out the best structure, but when you are starting out you won't likely have the need or the funds to do this. You can talk to the others involved with your business to decide on a structure that will work best. Try to learn current best practices based on what others are doing.

Action Steps:
Sketch out a draft of your own organizational structure.
1. Determine what skills you will need and list them out.
2. Group the skills together into job positions. For instance, all marketing skills would go under a "marketer" role. A member of a band would be marked by the instrument they play and so on.
3. Put the job positions into a chart (see Figure 5.1 for an organizational chart for the artist entrepreneur).

Compensation

Compensation can be a tricky thing to get right. An individual's true value might not be in line with his or her expectations, and who is to say what someone else is worth anyway? Reality dictates what kind of paycheck each person receives, and the perception of reality is sometimes distorted. Ultimately, pay will be determined as the result of a negotiation, and the laws of economics, such as supply and demand, will affect the outcome as well. Individuals with in-demand skills and talents can command higher pay, due to the fact that they can more easily find work elsewhere.

Determining the worth of someone's contribution can be straightforward or complex, depending on the role. A strategy I prefer, which is also endorsed by Ray Dalio, is to pay people fairly and then some. By being generous (when you can afford it), you send a strong signal that the work is valued, and the employee will almost always make an extra effort in order to reciprocate. Treat others the way you like to be treated.

Keep in mind that there is also a relationship between pay (reward) and risk. The business owner incurs greater liability if something goes wrong. This means they should be additionally compensated for taking the risks. What is reasonable and fair varies by organization. There are companies where the CEO is paid thousands of times what the average employee makes. Some would say this is fair (clearly, the board of directors believes so). Money paid to employees must usually come from revenues. Compensation can be a controversial subject. Regardless, it should always be addressed by leadership in a way that is fair and transparent.

Customer and Employee Policies

Every business should have some kind of an operating manual. The policies contained in the manual should be designed to ensure smooth operation and also fairness in dealings with customers and with each other. It's surprising how many startups neglect this important piece, perhaps thinking that things will work out and they can deal with issues as they arise. In reality, it's hard to craft coherent policies at the outset, and many policies will result from something that went wrong. Policies are supposed to help the company avoid repeating costly mistakes.

Have you ever been frustrated as a customer when trying to solve a problem you have with a company? Policies can be a source of endless aggravation to customers and employees alike. That's why it's so important to get them right. I believe that rules are made for the exceptions. Even when there is a policy in place, it should always be possible to escalate to a review of a specific situation by someone with the ability to override the policy. Policies are made to take care of most situations that could arise, but they can never cover everything. When something has gone wrong, the policy should allow for everyone to learn something from what happened, so that the problem doesn't reoccur.

It's hard to make good policy, but if leaders make it a logical outgrowth of the vision–mission–strategic imperative process, and the employees most affected have some say in the formulation of policy, the resultant buy-in will ensure that the policies are adhered to. In other words, policies should be created and enforced in a flexible enough way to accommodate situations that fall outside of the typical way things are done.

The same approach should apply to customers and clients. All business is personal, so treating clients like an individual and not a number will help them feel connected to the business. It's always easier to keep an existing customer than find a new one. While there are some people who are never satisfied, customer complaints should be viewed as an opportunity for learning, with the potential to strengthen your business. It's hard to endure criticism sometimes, but when you have complaining customers, clients, or employees you really should listen to them and consider how you might be able to make their experience better. Customers talk to each other, and social media can be a way for them to amplify their displeasure.

Taxes and Accounting

The answer to this question should always be: Yes. I like to sleep at night, so I always pay my taxes. After all, it's the law. Almost everyone will be audited at some point by the Internal Revenue Service (IRS), and when it is your turn, you needn't face undue anxiety or stress. This can only happen when you know you've done the right thing in the past. If you cheated on your taxes, even if you aren't caught, you'll always be burdened with the knowledge, and worried that you'll eventually get called to account. The consequences for hiding income are large and scary, such as big fines, or the garnishing of your future wages. Don't let this happen to you. Many people cut corners on their tax filings, but that doesn't mean it's the right thing to do. The law says you must declare all your income and pay taxes on it. Pay your taxes. All of them.

I remember my father used to say that having a tax bill was a good problem to have, because it meant you were making money. That's great advice. On the other hand, you shouldn't pay any more tax than you owe. Why would anyone give one extra cent to the government above what they're required to pay? Paying more taxes than required is a needless blunder.

The tax codes are exceedingly complex, so it isn't always easy to figure out how much you owe. There are also many layers of taxation, from the federal and state levels to county and city taxes. There is a social security tax and a Medicare tax on income (more on this next). There are sales taxes, gasoline taxes, excise taxes, for example, on boats and cars, property taxes, and licensing fees. Certain fees, like a vehicle registration, are considered a tax. On average, Americans pay more than 50 percent of their income in total taxes. They also receive great benefits as a result of paying taxes, such as roads, police and fire protection, schools, social security, and medical services in old age (at least for now).

Tax Freedom Day

Here is a concept I always found interesting and useful. If you add up all the taxes you pay on just income (Social Security, Medicare, Federal and State income taxes) and calculate it as a percentage of your gross pay, and then add up the number of days you work in a year, and apply the same percentage, you can put a date on the calendar and call it *Tax Freedom Day*. Here's an example:

Say you earn $50,000.00 a year from your job. Total taxes taken out of your paycheck before you see it amount to $20,000.00 or 40 percent of your gross pay. You work 50 weeks a year, or about 250 days and 40 percent of 250 days is 100 days. This means you will work the first 100 days of the year just to pay off your debt to the government, and that starting on day 101 you can keep all the money you earn. 100 days is 20 weeks, this means that for any given year your Tax Freedom Day will be on May 20, the first day of the 21st week.

Hiring an Accountant

Taxes for businesses and self-employed individuals can get really complicated, especially if you own assets like stocks and bonds, have an income property, have dependents, or earn your living as a freelancer. That's why most people hire an accountant to prepare their annual tax returns.

Finding the right accountant to work with isn't always easy. As with lawyers, it's better not to look for an accountant by searching on the internet. It's always better to get a referral from a trusted associate, a friend, or a family member. This gives you more accountability and leverage at the outset. Professionals care about referrals and will have an incentive to take great care of you, to avoid damaging their relationship with the referee. You can also ask a teacher for a referral.

You should talk to at least three different accountants before deciding who to hire. Remember that you are the customer and should expect to be treated like one. If someone seems too busy or is rude to you, don't hire them! Have a list of questions ready to ask, such as how much they charge and how their process works. You should expect that the accountant understands your small business needs and has some experience dealing with music and entertainment financial matters. They should know what kinds of tax deductions you are allowed to take and understand how you earn your money. You should explain your business to them and listen to what they say. They will also have questions for you, as they need to determine your needs and whether the relationship will be a good fit. Even if you don't hire the person, you are likely to learn something valuable from each interview.

I've had better results working with small independent accountants, as opposed to larger offices. The bigger firms have assistants do most of the work, who aren't as knowledgeable and often make mistakes. On the one hand, it might be nice to have more than one set of eyes review your returns, but I much prefer the personalized service that a one-person outfit provides. They also tend to cost less.

If you are happy with your accountant, you could ask them for a discount for referring others to them. Most musicians need to hire an accountant, and it isn't easy to find a good one. When all's said and done, your accountant's main job is to ensure you are paying all taxes you owe, and not a penny more. A knowledgeable and competent accountant can save you a lot more money than their fee.

Action Step:
Decide if you'll hire an accountant from a one-person office or a large office.

Liability Protection and Managing Risk

Earlier in this chapter we looked at the different types of business entities and how erecting a corporate veil can protect you from personal liability by separating your personal assets from those of your business. It's important to protect yourself this way, but you might also want to further protect your company from liability when things go wrong. Things inevitably do go wrong, and you could be dragged into court for any number of reasons. Fortunately, there are insurance products that can protect your business if this happens.

Risk is a part of life. You are more likely to die or be injured in an automobile crash than a plane crash, but that doesn't keep most of us from riding in cars or airplanes. Accepting a level of risk for your businesses is obligatory. Nonetheless, it's prudent to carefully consider all that could go wrong, and insure yourself for that when it's possible. That's why people buy life insurance when they have dependents. Some kinds of insurance, like auto insurance, are required by law. Following are two typical examples from my own recent experience.

I had organized a recording session in Boston that would take place on a specially outfitted 45-foot tour bus. I checked with the police about parking and was told I would need to secure a special permit from City Hall. When I contacted the proper office at City Hall, I was told that in order for them to issue a permit to me, I would need a bond. To get the bond, I would need to visit an insurance agent. The purpose of the bond was to make sure that if my bus caused any damage, it would be covered by an insurance policy. I purchased a $1 million bond for $50.00 and got my permit. A *bond* is simply another word for an insurance policy to cover a specific event.

When my band was hired to play a corporate event at a new hotel in Boston, the hotel required me to have special insurance to play there. If I couldn't get the insurance, I couldn't play there. Needless to say, I got the insurance.

There are liability policies anyone can buy for their business. In some cases, it might be more cost effective to buy liability insurance than to form a separate business entity like an LLC. It's worth talking to some insurance companies before making a decision about how to formalize your business entity. If you use an insurance broker, they can shop around for you at different companies to get you the best product and price. It's difficult to think about being in business without having some kinds of insurance. Insurance is a part of business, as it is a part of life.

Action Step:
Search for insurance companies that sell liability policies and decide if you want to speak with an insurance agent about options.

CHAPTER 7

Marketing, Branding, and Sales: How to Find Your Fan Base and Promote Your Music

Now that we know what's in a business plan and how to create our business entity, let's turn again to marketing, branding, and sales. They are the lifeblood of your music business.

This chapter will give some ideas about how to begin to market yourself and start earning money with your music. You should gain an elementary understanding of what marketing and sales is, how they differ, and how they are related. Let's dive right in and try to make sense of it all.

If you ask the average person you meet, most wouldn't know the difference between marketing and sales. *Marketing* refers to strategies and tactics designed to identify and appeal to consumers. *Sales* involves the exchange of money from a consumer to a provider for a service or product. Sometimes, people think that marketing involves some psychological voodoo to make you buy something, and that salespeople use nefarious methods to trick you into spending too much money on things you don't really need. In a sense, they are right. The literature on sales and marketing proscribes myriad techniques to pry your hard-earned cash from your wallet using inherent cognitive biases most people don't realize they have. A whole academic field, *behavioral economics*, exists and examines why people make financial decisions that are against their best interests.

At some level, every band and musician understands that the key to their future success involves marketing. Success in the music industry goes hand in hand with fame, which by definition requires that lots of people know about you and your music. To further complicate the issue, luck and timing also play into whether you break through to fame and success, or will fail. You might have the most amazing band, and play incredibly great music, but if nobody knows about you, or can remember your name, you won't get very far. Music marketing is the process and set of techniques for making potential fans aware of your music.

Although many people don't realize marketing and sales are two different things, truthfully, sales cannot happen without marketing, and the goal of marketing is to drive sales. The words *promoting* and *marketing* are sometimes used interchangeably. *Branding* is also not the same as marketing, though the two are closely related. *Positioning* refers to how you embed your brand in the minds of your prospects, especially regarding their perceived needs or wants, and in relation to your competition. Positioning your brand in the market is as much art as it is science, and it's difficult for the musician starting out to know where to begin. There are a lot of terms being thrown around, so you'll need to do some of your own research and study to make it all work for you.

Research into thinking applies directly to marketing. An understanding of psychology is important for anyone seeking to understand consumer behavior and marketing. So is understanding business analytics and the promise of big data, machine learning, and artificial intelligence in social media data analytics. These topics are bigger than the scope of this book, but I'll help you to see the big picture and provide some useful insights about marketing in the music industry.

Artist Marketing Concept: Bridging the Gap Between Creative Zone and End User

Artists and musicians are used to thinking about their work in creative terms. We're very comfortable living our life in this zone, working to improve our skills and abilities, while building on our natural talent. We work diligently at musical skills, practicing difficult passages on our instrument; we focus on perfecting our arpeggios, proper ergonomic posture, breathing (for vocalists), improvising, composing, and countless other technical aspects that, when taken together, serve to elevate our creative faculties to world-class levels.

We know that music is a competitive arena and that building ourselves up in this way is a terrific (and usually, fun) investment. After all, this is why we were attracted to the idea of doing music in the first place. We admired others who had achieved great musical heights, and made a decision to do this ourselves. This is all exactly as it should be.

However, there is another zone that I will call the *end user*, for lack of a better term. This zone is likely to be less familiar and less comfortable to most creative individuals. I'll explain.

If you ask most musicians who their music is for, they might answer "for anyone who likes good music." After all, if you are making good music, anyone who likes good music should like your music, right? It makes perfect sense, and it's a legitimate answer, perhaps as good as any. However, this answer won't work for marketing purposes. When creating a marketing plan, the first thing you should consider is your audience. Who are they? Where are they? How will you reach them? What do they want? Why do they want it?

There is more to this than initially meets the eye. Describing your music and what you do in a way that will not only appeal to an audience, but make them do what you want them to do (buy a ticket and come to your gig) is as much a science as it is an art. Effective marketing requires deep understanding of the specific audience you want to reach, or the target. The question of who you create your music for leads us to the science of *demography*, the study of populations and their characteristics.

Target Demographic, Profiling

We're going to build on the work we did on your target market in an earlier chapter. It's important to think about the *core* of your fans, so we have something to aim for. Let's say you imagine that most people listening to your music might range from 16 to 32 years old; this doesn't mean there wouldn't be an 80-year-old or an 8-year-old who also likes your music. But we would call those people *outliers,* as they do not make up the bulk of your fans and as a group aren't as likely to spend their hard-earned cash on your music.

Action Steps:

Answer the following questions.

Besides age, we should think about your prospects' other characteristics.

1. Are there more men or women?
2. Where do they live, in which countries or cities?
3. What race are they, or what religion, if any, do they follow?
4. What TV shows, movies, video games, or sports do they watch?
5. Where do they shop for clothes?
6. Do they go to restaurants, and if so, which ones?
7. Do they belong to a gym?
8. What about their income and education levels?
9. Do they follow the news or read magazines?
10. Which news outlets or magazines?
11. Which social media platforms do they use?

Harness your imagination.

As you consider all this, you could invent a fictitious individual that will represent your core fan base. This is called a *demographic profile*. Here's an example:

> Jim is a 26-year-old resident of Cincinnati with a bachelor's degree in economics from the state college. He works full time as a business analyst at a regional bank and is in a committed relationship with Anna who also works in a bank. They share a rented three-bedroom apartment in a close-in suburban neighborhood and commute to their jobs in the city. They like to meet after work for drinks and dinner a few times a week, frequenting a variety of local pubs or mid-to-upscale restaurants. They attend the Episcopalian Church and their combined income is about $95,000.00 annually. On weekends they will occasionally buy tickets to a concert, either to see a national act or some other regional band they both like. They occasionally go to a sporting event or a movie, and spend other nights watching movies or shows on Netflix when they aren't going out.

This could continue with more details, but we now start to get a picture of what the target demographic looks like. You should create multiple profiles, perhaps between three and six in total. This is a fun exercise because you are describing your future fans. Let your creative juices flow.

Action Step:
Write your own demographic profile for a future fan or customer.

The next step is to look at our prospective audience's psychological makeup.

Psychographic Imaging

When we talk about "psychographics" in relation to a market, we're referring to people's attitudes, aspirations, problems, and how they think overall. Questions to consider when creating your psychographic profiles:

- What do your prospects talk to their friends about?
- What are they worried about?
- What keeps them up at night?
- What would they like to learn more about?
- Are they passionate about any causes?

Look at the profiles you've already created and breathe life into them. Real people have real problems; what are your prospects' most thorny issues? The next step is to create a *psychographic profile* for your customer.

All people have specific needs, whether real or imagined. They also want certain things. Get inside your prospects' heads.

Answer these questions:

- Do they care about status? Having fun? Or are they more concerned with saving the planet?
- What do they really want more than anything else?
- Are they feeling conflicted about certain issues?
- Perhaps they have some things in common with you. If so, what are those things?

Remember that we need them to open their wallet if we want to get paid for our work. We might also want them to do other things or to change how they think. This means we need to communicate to them with our branding and marketing materials in a language they understand. This is the true job of the marketer: to communicate to your target audience precisely what your brand stands for in the world.

Since you want them to know about you and remember your name, your image identity materials (branding) must resonate with them meaningfully. Marketing is a psychological undertaking that seeks to influence people in their decision making. To connect with your audience, you must know and understand them, their cares, worries, and their psyche. Then you can consider how your music might appeal to them or help them, and influence their actions. This is what psychographic profiling is all about.

Consider that you have been marketed to your whole life, and start paying attention to the brands that grab your attention, and how they do it. Using demographic and psychographic profiling, you'll gain an understanding of the people you need to reach, and how to craft your message. Keep this information in the front of your mind as you create and produce your music and your marketing materials. You're not making your music for just anybody, you're making it for *somebody*.

Action Steps:
Answer the aforementioned questions. Write the answers down to add to your customer profiles.

Marketing Artistry, and More Marketing

As I've shown, marketing is a critical function of business. Aspiring music careerists should build skills and understanding through careful study and observation. Starting with demographic and psychographic profiling and research, you will use your newfound marketing skills to identify and target your future fan base.

Fortunately, there are tons of great resources out there for learning about marketing. I realized early on that music is a fashion business, so I got some textbooks to read on fashion marketing. Since music is also part of the entertainment, media, film, video game, events, sports, and advertising fields, you can find informative books and blogs about marketing in those areas that also apply to music. There are excellent books on marketing psychology, like the classic *Positioning: The Battle for Your Mind* by

Al Ries and Jack Trout (McGraw-Hill, 1981) and the Malcolm Gladwell bestseller *The Tipping Point* (Little, Brown, and Co., 2002). There are also great books about the music industry available that include sections on marketing, such as those written by Bobby Borg, Peter Spellman, Donald Passman, and Ari Herstand. You can find more reading suggestions by asking your teachers or a librarian, following blogs, or searching online.

You could go to a university and get an MBA in music and entertainment marketing. Sports marketing is similar to music marketing. Using the internet and other resources, you can learn all about social media marketing, which is constantly evolving. I found it helpful to view the music business through the lens of all these other connected industries and to undertake a lengthy and serious study of marketing and how it applies to music. I recommend that anyone seeking a music career get serious with learning how to be an effective marketer. Your musical artistry will be an asset to your learning, since marketing is a creative endeavor at its core.

Bridging the Gap: DIWO (Do It With Others)

Let's return now to the point I made earlier in this chapter: how to bridge the gap between our creative zone and the end user. Shift your thinking from the mostly creative aspects of musicianship, to the more analytical work of preparing to market our music and ourselves. Preparing to launch your music business as a career takes a lot of work. The good news is that you don't have to do it alone.

You've likely heard about DIY marketing or *Do It Yourself*. This phrase first entered the music industry's collective consciousness during the 1990s, notably when singer-songwriter Ani DiFranco from Buffalo, NY, took on all the aspects of managing her career and her business, forming her own label, Righteous Babe Records. The term *indie artist*, short for independent artist, became a buzzword representing a new ethos and way of doing business that rejected the previous industry domination by the major record labels. Indie artists sought to maintain total control over all aspects of their career, from creative choices and the recording process, to touring and album cover artwork.

DIY signals an evolution of the music business independent (indie) artist model, but it's a misnomer. Indie artists rely on the services and talents of other professionals, sometimes called *intermediaries,* such as session musicians, audio engineers, producers, accountants, lawyers, photographers, stylists, and tour managers. With the indie model, these intermediaries typically report directly to the artist, instead of a label or manager.

That's why I prefer the term DIWO, or *Do It With Others.* With DIWO, some intermediaries might contribute consistently over time, like musicians in the band. Some might only come in for a day's work here and there, like a photographer or a stylist. Team-building means finding and choosing the right people, and then managing the professional relationships. The team members are usually paid by the artist.

Assembling and leading teams is a critical function of executive leadership. It's never too early to start assembling your team. Look around you and consider who might be able to help you or collaborate with you in some way. If you're in school, you will be surrounded by others who are also developing their careers. Many will have skills complimentary to your own. Talk to everyone you meet, and be friendly. Regularly put your ideas forward to others, and share your thoughts about the future. Watch how people respond. Your enthused fellow students will be your future collaborators.

For others you need, you should ask teachers, mentors, or other authority figures for referrals. It's always good to get referrals to entertainment attorneys, and share your music with them. Some of them can pitch your music to others in the industry. You will need an attorney to review any contracts you are eventually offered, so it's smart to build those relationships early on. When you set up your business entity, and start earning money from your music, you will need a lawyer and an accountant. They will be key players on the team you're building.

Whether you think from a DIY perspective or are looking to progress to the majors, you will need other professionals in your corner.

Differentiation Strategy

I'm going to share one of the biggest "secrets" with you about success in any industry. This secret actually hides in plain view, where most people can't see it. Success is not usually random, the result of dumb luck, or some other mysterious factor. Luck does play a role, but the majority of successful people achieve their professional and life goals through deliberate and strategic action. They plan carefully and execute on their plans exceptionally well. They work incredibly hard at it. And, they probably also have some luck.

By the way, what looks like an overnight success may have taken 15 years. A big break is always the result of lots of little breaks. This is the reality. I'm going to share a secret of success in the music industry with you. And guess what? it's related, again, to marketing.

Let's conduct a thought exercise. Think of a well-known artist, living or dead, preferably a household name (one that most people will know). Suggestions: Madonna, Prince, Katy Perry, Taylor Swift, The Rolling Stones, Lady Gaga, or Stevie Wonder. Think about the images you see in your mind when you consider these famous artists. What kind of image is the artist trying to cultivate? With the Rolling Stones, it might be a rebellious "bad boy" kind of image, with sexual undertones. The album names, art, and logo (Sticky Fingers, big lips, and tongue) are also an attempt to brand their desired image into your mind. What about the difference between Lady Gaga and Taylor Swift? Or Prince and Elton John? The artists themselves would have very specific answers about the image they work to convey. They know exactly what sets them apart from all the others. They don't have to guess. They know.

Pick any famous artist. When you say their name, an image immediately pops up in your head, doesn't it? The precise image might be slightly different for you than for me, but that doesn't matter, because they will be similar. Whether or not you are a fan of the artist is immaterial. The important thing is that you recognize their name immediately and there's an image that pops up in your mind.

The image is designed to lodge itself in our minds and to appeal to our preferences and taste. It's created with purpose. The artist likely has a team of marketing and publicity people who work hard every day to put that image in your mind. This might sound like a radical idea, but it's true. The image occupies a rung of a ladder in your mind that ranks artists according to your own preferences, and of course the artist marketing team wants their client to be on the top rung. They designed this image to appeal to your emotions. Crafty, indeed.

Here is the success secret I promised I'd share with you. There is one question everyone needs to answer eventually:

What makes you different from everyone else who does what you do?

If you are a songwriter, how are you different from all the other songwriters? If you are a guitarist, what sets you apart from all others who play guitar? Successful artists know the answer to this question and can articulate it clearly.

Answering this question is not easy, and it could take you some years. But don't worry. You can get started without knowing the answer right away. There are a few people who just know, and seem to have always known, but most people need some time to figure it out. Once you have the answer, you still need to communicate it to your prospective fan base and others in the industry, which also presents a challenge.

Knowing what makes you different and communicating it to your prospects is called your *differentiation strategy*. If you are writing your business plan, you will need to address this in multiple sections of the plan. Don't let the fact that it's difficult scare you. If it was easy, everyone would be doing it. Understanding your differentiation strategy gives an advantage in business and is a key to success in music or any industry.

Action Step:
Write down what makes you and your music different from others who do what you do.

Is There a Need?

You'll also need to find out if there is an actual need for what you do. Do you think the world needs more songwriters? Do we really need more guitar players? When I ask students whether they think there's a need for what they do, some aren't quite sure. If you want to make your living doing something, whatever it is, that means someone must be willing to pay you to do it. Why would anyone pay for something they don't need? Therefore, if you expect to get paid for what you do, you should make sure there's actually a need for it.

If there's no need, that doesn't mean you shouldn't do it. It just means you'll either have to create a need, or you should do it as a hobby. How do we know if there is a need? We have to research the market. My decades of research have shown me that in the music industry there's always a need. Everyone is always looking for the next big thing. No matter how many singers, songwriters, producers, or guitar players there are, there will always be room for one more. If you also believe this, research where the need is and then market to it, using the techniques in this chapter.

Branding: What's in a Name?

One of the most important business decisions you must make is choosing the name of your business. Many musicians and artists use their birth name, but others choose a modified version of their name, or they might choose a name they think is more memorable.

Bob Dylan's birth name is Robert Zimmerman. He chose Dylan as his last name to honor Beat Generation poet Dylan Thomas, with whom he identified. Sting's real name is Gordon Sumner. Elton John's birth name is Reginald Kenneth Dwight. Bruce Springsteen's birth name is Bruce Springsteen. When he signed his first record deal, the record label wanted him to change it and he refused.

What if you are a rock vocalist and your real name is Mick Jagger? Sorry, but you will have to change it. If you start advertising yourself as Mick Jagger, even if it's your real name, The Rolling Stones' Mick Jagger's people will eventually tell you to stop, because from their perspective you are fooling audiences and trying to make money off his (trademarked) name. When is it time to trademark a name? Best to ask a lawyer about this. There are other, less expensive ways to protect the use of your name, as we discussed in the previous chapter.

One of the toughest things about finding a good name for your band or your business is that most of the good names are already taken. If you thought of it, there's a good chance that someone else did too and beat you to it. You can check if the website domain is available; that is usually a pretty good indicator of whether or not a name is in use. A name using a made-up word can be the solution, since it's unlikely someone else already has it. Think about companies like Verizon, Comcast, Xerox, Kodak, and Kleenex. All are made-up names that stick in the memory.

The most important thing about your name is that it's easy for people to remember. It should be "sticky" in the mind, so that people can quickly recall it without too much effort. Have you ever seen an entertaining commercial, only to realize immediately afterwards you couldn't remember the name of the product or company? That's not a good ad, and it's probably not a memorable product name. There are people who specialize in just thinking up names for businesses, products, movies, or bands, and they get paid a lot of money for doing it. It's absolutely crucial to come up with just the right name.

Choosing a name is an exercise in branding every new business faces. Sometimes a tag line will also accompany the name. Think: "Nike, Just Do It," or "Fly the Friendly Skies of United." A lot of careful thought goes into designing a logo, and selecting images, color schemes, and fonts, with the goal of positioning the brand so it's immediately recognizable and memorable to the target demographic. We'll return to naming challenges in Chapter 14 when we discuss how to set up your own music publishing company.

Action Steps:
Come up with potential names.
 1. Write down a list of 10 possible names.
 2. Check the WHOIS database to see if the website URL (or domain) has already been purchased. Check the TESS database to see if anyone has already trademarked the name.
 3. Based on what you discover, make adjustments to the names on your list and cross some off.
 4. Narrow down your list to three to five and then request feedback from trusted associates.

A Magic Branding Formula: Image Identity Materials

In my work consulting with young artists and musicians, they usually want to know what steps they should take next to develop their career. Not knowing where to start feels understandably overwhelming, since there's so much to do. A feeling of helplessness sets in, and of course they are looking for specific direction.

In the context of artist development, we can bring order to the chaos. If you've defined your target demographic, you can start creating your image identity materials. I've invented a formula for this. I call it **I²M** (pronounce: *I squared M*). Carefully branding yourself and your music is the logical next step in your self-marketing.

It's best to organize and then prioritize your work. I like to build and test models for everything I do in my own career. I express my formula for artist development as in Figure 7.1.

So: *Image Identity materials*, multiplied by *Branding*, plus *Resonance with target demographic*, equals *Market access*.

This is a simplification, as any formula needs to be. I could use other, more complex formulas to describe the demographic of the target market, viral marketing techniques with social media analytics, or to model fan engagement with streaming platforms, but this simple equation will serve our purposes for now. I like this kind of simple equation because it puts the focus on what we can do right now, and why we need to do it. I'll briefly explain each part of the equation.

What Is I²M?

I abbreviated *Image Identity Materials* this way to highlight that your image and identity are intertwined, and each supports the other in a synergistic way. Image identity materials are designed to broadcast your image and include, but are not limited to:

- Artist/band name
- Professional video
- Photos, images
- Color schemes, artwork
- Special fonts
- Websites
- Social media pages
- Recordings

- Artist bio
- Attire
- Press clippings
- "One Page"
- Logo
- Posters, flyers
- Merchandise
- Stage set design

$$I^2 M (B + R^t) = M^a$$

WHERE:
I^2 ("I squared") = Image Identity
M = Materials

B = Branding
R^t = Resonance with target demographic
M^a = Market access

Figure 7.1 Artist development formula

Your visual materials are super important because people decide in a nano-second whether they like you based on visual impact, whereas it takes a bit longer for them to process the music aurally or by reading text. In the digital era, you need compelling visual images or people won't likely click a link to listen to your music, watch a video, or buy tickets to see you perform. Images should quickly define who you are (your identity), and communicate why a potential listener and fan should know about you. Most importantly, your I^2M needs to appeal to the viewer, and cleverly convey what your music is all about.

(B + R^t) Is Branding and Resonance With Your Target Market

Branding used in this context refers to the execution of your image identity strategy. Branding encompasses how you craft your messages, the quality of your materials, memorability of your name, instant recognition of your logo, catchy color scheme, and expressive fonts, photographs and art, along with any other unifying visual elements that create impact. It's also about the values your brand stands for. Successful branding is crucial to the success of any marketing campaign. Your branding tells your back story.

Resonance is simply how well your materials are received by your target demographic. With social media marketing, resonance is a measure of how many people access and share curated content. When content is released and quickly gets millions of views, this is because many people like it and want to share it with others in their networks. Highly resonant memes and videos are quickly viewed and shared by millions. The ultimate in resonance is virality. We use the term *viral* to describe when content gets shared widely and quickly across social networks.

When your branding materials resonate with your target market, it will give you *access* to the *market*. This formula is a powerful tool for gaining traction with your marketing as an artist.

In the next chapter, we will take a closer look at the image identity materials artists and bands use to promote themselves and their music, specifically, the Electronic Promo Kit, or EPK.

CHAPTER 8

Music Marketing: How to Make an EPK (Electronic Promo Kit)

An EPK Is Your First Impression

First impressions are important in business. A solid and concise *Electronic Promo Kit* (EPK) helps you to make the right first impression. Prospective partners and A&Rs want to see what you show your intended audience, but they have different interests than fans, and will be looking for certain things at first glance. They will want to listen to a few tracks and learn more about your brand. They are typically very busy and won't have much time, so it's crucial you put your best foot forward. You should have your best work right up front, since they will assume anything you show them is the best you can do.

They need to be able to understand the most important points quickly and easily, so you should give them just enough to do that and not more. Your EPK should make it easy for them and should have no excess materials or fluff. For your first impression, your EPK is more than a calling card. It's your ultimate marketing tour-de-force.

What's in an EPK, and Who Is It for?

An EPK is your digital portfolio delivered over the Web and is designed mainly to promote a band or artist to others in the industry. As discussed in Chapter 7, we call these industry professionals *intermediaries* because they insert themselves into the artist development, marketing, or business development process. Some examples of intermediaries:

- Lawyer
- Manager
- Accountant
- Record label A&R (Artist and Repertoire)

- Booking agent
- Promoter
- Publicist

Additional types of intermediaries who will have interest in your EPK might include:

- Producer
- Music supervisor
- Tour manager
- Venue owner/manager
- Festival director
- Video producer

- Music director/conductor
- Session musician
- Stylist
- Photographer
- Engineer
- Web designer

This is not an all-inclusive list, but it's clear that just about anyone you will want to work with wants to see your EPK first. Their goal at outset is to get a very quick and clear understanding of your music and to see how you market yourself. They want to know where you are in your business development process, and what drives you.

In Chapter 7, I walked you through clarifying your target audience. Your EPK should make clear who that audience is and how you intend to reach them, and should clearly communicate how and why your music and persona resonate with your intended fan base. The goal is straightforward, but it's not a simple task. A lot of thought and care goes into crafting an effective EPK, as it reflects on your professionalism, preparedness, talent, ability, and commitment. It's worth your time and effort to make it as good as possible, since your music career could depend on it.

Begin your EPK creation process by thinking carefully about who will view it. If your goals are to get a major label record deal and a big-time manager, your EPK will look different than if your target is an indie label or a booking agent. As you design your EPK and work on the materials to include, think about who will see it, and what you want them to do.

Action Steps:

1. Write down your goals for your EPK. Consider who you want to see it, and describe the impression it should make on them.
2. Next, consider what you think they will want to see in your EPK. Write that down, too.

Take your time with this, because the answers will guide the foundation of your EPK and all of the pieces that follow.

Let's see what is inside your EPK. The most basic version might contain the following:

- Recorded music
- Photos and artwork
- Artist bio
- Videos
- Press clippings
- Quotes
- Links to social media
- Crowdfunding
- Contact info

Think of it as your musical resume which lives online. You want it to be easy to find and easy to navigate. I'll describe each component in turn, mention some hosting options, and suggest how you can get it in front of the people you want to see it. This aligns with the I²M branding formula from the last chapter.

Recorded Music

Sound recordings that used to require long hours in a recording studio can now be accomplished in much less time using a laptop computer with quality peripherals and software. Whether in your bedroom or in a fully equipped recording studio, you should do whatever it takes to create excellent recordings, since it's important for advancing your career. Listeners will assume it's the best you can produce, so make sure that it really is your best work.

Quality recordings make your music more accessible and enjoyable to listen to. Listeners will notice and appreciate you care enough about your music to record it properly. Your recordings can live in your EPK as audio files or be hosted on another platform, such as SoundCloud. If you opt for the latter, embed the file in your EPK so the listener doesn't need to leave the hosting site to listen.

Photos and Artwork

The same advice applies to your photos and artwork. Buy the best quality you can afford. It pays to hire professionals and, if you're a student, you may be able to get a discount or even barter for these services. You could offer a photography or art student some music lessons in exchange for their work, which they could also use for their own portfolios. Promotional photos (a.k.a. *promo pics*) should be style-appropriate. The setting and attire might look quite different for an aspiring opera diva than a metal band. Choose your settings to create the right "vibe" or ambience for your brand. Artwork can be album art, website page designs, logos, or any graphics that represent your brand image.

If you are planning to use live performance shots, have the photographer include the audience and their reactions in their camera angles. Seeing enthusiastic audience members makes a stronger impression than seeing shots of just the performers on the stage without the audience in view. Your photographer will need full access to the stage during your performance to get shots that include the audience.

Action Steps:
1. Find a photographer.
2. Note what band photography you've liked a lot.
3. Ask your musician friends for recommendations.
4. Make a list of three to five photographers you can research and talk to later.
5. Be sure to choose a setting that reflects your brand image.

Artist Bio

The bio is where you get to tell your backstory and explain to your prospective audience why they should be interested in you and your music. It doesn't need to be very long, but it does need to be well written, without spelling, grammar, capitalization, punctuation, or other errors. Above all else, it should be interesting, and tell the reader what you want them to know about you and your music. Bios can be humorous, serious, tongue-in-cheek, and even fictitious, as long as it is clear you aren't being deceptive.

The bio should not be too long; usually two to three paragraphs are sufficient. If you wish to do a long-form bio as well, you could include both versions. If your audience is international, you might want to offer versions in different languages.

Action Steps:
Write your artist bio. Or, retrieve the bio you used for your business plan. You might end up making changes to it for the EPK's purposes, yet it will give a start.

Videos

Although not all EPKs use videos, I recommend using video if you have quality live video that shows your music in a positive light. If you have professionally produced concert or music videos, that's always great to have in your EPK, as long as it shows you at your very best. If your videos are grainy, unfocused, poorly lighted, or otherwise not professionally produced, it's probably better not to include them.

Tip: As with live performance photographs, always include the audience with your camera angles. The best performance videos show enthusiastic audience reactions. Make sure your videos have excellent audio as well.

Press Clippings, Quotes

If you don't have any press articles or quotes from other influential people to put in your EPK, make it your mission to get some. Think like a publicist: Find writers and reviewers at local news outlets, and make friends with them. Interview some well-known musicians, talk to radio people— be resourceful and you can generate the buzz you need. It takes some effort and strategic thinking, but it's worth it. Having positive comments from believable people and news articles about you gives you extra credibility, can help you attract an audience, and is evidence you are a musical force to be reckoned with.

Social Media Links

A&R departments at major labels aren't only interested in obvious talent or good music. To offer a deal, prospective labels and intermediaries want to see that you've already cultivated loyal and dedicated fans. The best way to show strong potential is to have an audience already in place. Growing and maintaining a social media presence using frequent direct engagement with fans is very convincing when it's done with authenticity and integrity. It should never be faked. Buying likes and follows is a bad idea, which experienced industry people will quickly see through, and they will write you off for it. Your following and interactions online must be verifiably real.

Free platforms you can use to build your following include Instagram, YouTube, Twitter, SoundCloud, TikTok, Reddit, and others. LinkedIn is extremely important because all the music industry people use it, so you should definitely have a credible and completely filled out profile on LinkedIn. Engaging actively with your fans on social media is a requirement for all aspiring artists and bands in today's music industry.

Labels look for evidence of your fan base and want to see you are already earning money with your music. One award-winning A&R representative I know lists his requirements for consideration on his website, stating right up front that great talent and music isn't enough to be eligible for submission. He asks that, in addition to great talent and image, artist bio, and proof of regular live shows, that candidates have 30,000 Spotify streams per month, 70,000 Twitter followers, and a YouTube video with half a million views. He requests that artists do not contact him until they can meet those requirements and can also prove they are already earning money from their music.

Your EPK is the place to show off all your online stats. Music business people pay close attention to data analytics. They will want to see that you have a strong social media presence, where your followers are located, and how often they engage with you online. For your online social presence, build it and they will come.

Crowdfunding

You may not be quite that far along with your following, or your goals may not be to sign with a major label, and that's perfectly fine. Regardless, you should strive to show through your EPK that you have the ability to generate strong interest in your music as an independent artist or band. One oft-overlooked way to do that is through a successful crowdfunding campaign.

Besides the obvious goal of raising funds to record or tour, successful crowdfunding is powerful proof that you appeal to a real audience. More artists should consider crowdfunding as a "proof of concept" for their music business prospects. There are many types of crowdfunding models artists can use; KickStarter, Indiegogo, and Patreon are some popular choices. I recommend investigating this further and showing the results in your EPK, if you are successful with it.

Where Should Your EPK Live?

The EPK can be a standalone file, like a zip file. The advantage of this is that you can send it as an enclosure, and the recipient won't need to be connected to the internet to view and listen after they've downloaded it. Many artists and bands will make their EPK available online to anyone who wants to check it out, though this isn't a requirement. If you do this, you can send the URL as a link via e-mail, text, or chat, and the EPK might also appear in search results from search engines like Google or Bing.

Some music aggregators like SonicBids or ReverbNation are created specifically to host your EPK; other places to host include your own website or a full service platform like Bandzoogle. An advantage of an aggregator is you can use it to integrate other business functions such as merchandising, ticketing, designing your website, blogging, and e-mail marketing campaigns. They can also streamline looking for gigs, integrate your calendar into your EPK, link to the venues you play, handle ticketing and payments, and help you license your recordings for use in visual media. They might also have an automated e-mail marketing function to stay in contact with fans en masse using a newsletter, for example. Most aggregator sites charge a monthly subscription fee.

Action Step:
Shop around to find the online platform for your EPK that most closely suits your needs and budget.

When MySpace was new in the 1990s, I wondered whether musicians needed a website of their own to promote their music. I still wonder the same thing. While some artists use websites, others choose to promote themselves on social media platforms such as Facebook, Instagram, Twitter, LinkedIn, Pinterest, Clubhouse, or TikTok. Other artists choose to use music streaming services such as Pandora or Spotify as their promotional home base. Music aggregators like Sonicbids, Bandzoogle, TuneCore, ReverbNation, and CD Baby all allow artists to quickly and easily upload and host their music and marketing materials.

With so many digital channels available to reach your audience, it's easy to be confused or overwhelmed by choices. People are busy, and attention spans are short. When you approach a record label, a booking agent, or an entertainment lawyer, what do you want them to see? How will your audience find you? What is guaranteed to grab and keep their interest? What are the right choices? Don't feel too overwhelmed; just inform yourself the best you can, and then choose whatever seems right.

A professional looking EPK allows you to quickly and clearly show your best work to others, while telling them why they should want to hear you and work with you. Since you only get one chance to make a first impression, it's important to dedicate the utmost care and thoughtfulness to create your EPK as the ultimate ninja marketing tool for you and your music.

CHAPTER 9

Networking in the Music Industry

You went to a party or gathering where there were people who could be helpful to you in your career. Maybe you passed out your business cards and told them about what you do. Then you went home and waited, hoping they would reach out to you with an opportunity or to introduce you to other helpful people. And then…nothing. Not a peep. Has this happened to you?

We often hear how crucial it is to network for success. This is true in every industry, and especially in the music business. We've all heard: It's not what you know, it's who you know. I would add: It's who you know that knows what you do, and who *they* know. Actively growing your network is only the beginning.

To reach decision makers, it's not just important to make connections. You must also know how to *leverage* your network. Knowing the right people gets you where you want to go, if you have the talent and skills to back it up. You can be great at what you do, but if nobody knows it, you're toast. The most successful people tend to be master networkers.

What Many People Get Wrong About Networking

Networking is an overused buzzword. I've noticed that few people really understand networking or know how to do it effectively. It's more than going to parties and handing out business cards. Yes, it's important to meet people face-to-face when you can, but nowadays most networking happens online, starting with the various social media sites. But sitting all day staring at your screen and tapping on your keyboard doesn't guarantee results, either.

True networking is more than just meeting new people. It means offering value, while building mutually beneficial professional relationships that last. It's about making yourself useful to others with no expectation of anything in return. Collecting business cards for your virtual rolodex or building a large following online might help you, but only if you know what to do next. At the outset, cultivate a deeper understanding of what networking is, how it's done, and how to leverage your network once it's in place. Then, practice and improve.

Some people are just natural networkers, it seems they are born to it. The rest of us must study, learn techniques, get organized, and apply what we learned. I think of networking as a game, or a puzzle with many pieces, all connected. Decide to attack the networking game with diligence and persistence, and you will succeed.

Where to Start: Sourcing

What some people think of as networking, the initial part of the game, I call *sourcing*. For example: I often drive a different route home from my job. I look for new bars, restaurants, and nightclubs about to open. Places always close down and new ones open in the same space. When I spot a new venue opening, I go inside to look for the manager or owner. I'll ask if they are considering live music as a tool to get customers in the door and keep them there. I might be able to book my band into a new room, and be first to play there. If it works, these gigs turn into long-term engagements. The advantage of being first is huge, and I can build a solid partnership with the club to help them get established.

Always look for innovative ways to meet new people, and learn about them. Initiate the conversation. Try to help them succeed in some way. Tell them about yourself. Make new friends. This is the beginning of true networking. When you help others, usually they also want to help you. This is not difficult, but you do have to abandon all fear of talking to people, and extend yourself to them in a helping way.

Build your list of contacts by seeking out those you want in your network, and then connecting with them. You can meet people anywhere—parties and events, meet new people who share your interests in the music industry, and make a new friend. Besides events and meetings, there are conferences, concerts, meetups, community functions, and of course live music clubs or hangouts where musicians gather.

Rules of the Game

There are some proven techniques for sourcing and building your network. Always have a game plan when you attend networking events. For example, a rule I use is not spending too much time talking with any one person. I limit time spent with each, so I don't miss out on meeting others. I also prefer to attend solo, so I don't waste time hanging out with the person I came with. If I go together with someone, we agree in advance to split up for most of the time we're there.

A few more tips:

1. When you pass out your card, make sure to also get the other person's. That puts you in control of following up. If you don't get their contact, you're leaving the follow-up to them.
2. Most people won't follow up, because they either forget, are lazy, or aren't avid networkers (many people just aren't great at it).
3. In case they don't have a card, carry a small notepad and pen so you can write down their contact info.
4. Make it your mission to leave with a set amount of new contacts, say five or ten.

Be a Strategic Networker: A Few Tips

It's important to develop networking strategies that work. Here are some I use.

1. Spend more time asking questions than talking about yourself. People like to talk about themselves, so find ways to draw them out. Don't worry if you are shy or introverted. With a small effort you can overcome your initial resistance. The key is to get them talking, so you can listen. Listening to people is a form of love.
2. Prepare a short statement ready to tell people what you do, where you're from, plus anything you'd like them to know about you.

This is your *elevator pitch* (since you should finish in the time it takes for an elevator ride). After you introduce yourself, have a few leading questions prepared to draw them out. If you don't monopolize the conversation, they will be more likely to remember you and like you.

3. Eat beforehand, keeping hands free (and clean) to shake hands. I don't want to waste time eating and don't want to speak with food in my mouth. I'm very careful about drinking alcohol; I don't want to get so inebriated that I might do or say something I regret. I choose a soft drink and hold it in my left hand. This leaves my right hand free and gives me something to do with my left hand that isn't awkward.

4. Always dress appropriately for the event and wear comfortable shoes, as you'll be standing around for a few hours.

You can find plenty more tips in the many networking blogs and articles found online. Now, prepare yourself to go get those important names and contacts.

Sourcing via the Web: LinkedIn

Take your sourcing game online. LinkedIn is the premier social platform for business networking. Have a credible LinkedIn profile and learn to use all the features.

1. To start, fill out every section fully
2. Join some groups
3. Post comments and likes
4. Share relevant content
5. Add connections
6. Give and get endorsements and written recommendations
7. Research companies and new connections

Other social platforms are also useful, but LinkedIn is the best game in town for business and it's free. Use it. Once you connect with people online, start the conversation.

Sourcing is only the beginning of the game. You are getting your pieces on the board, but you still need to connect everything. Now it's time to get organized in your networking efforts. Now that you've made the connections, you must leverage them to reach your goals. Learn to apply the strategies and techniques that work best for you.

Getting Organized: Have Specific Goals, Systemize and Leverage

Sourcing connections is the beginning, let's look at the next steps.

After the event, you hang your jacket in the closet, where it stays for a few months. Later, you take it out, feel in the pocket, and find a business card. You can't remember the person, so you toss it in the trash. This used to happen to me; don't let it happen to you. Leveraging your network means setting some goals, creating a system, and sticking to it. This requires organizational skill, the ability to learn from mistakes, a positive attitude, and most of all, persistence.

Think of your network as a living, breathing thing. It needs tending and care, and you are the caretaker. As it grows, you must direct its path. You will need a system for this, and there are some outstanding ready-made ones available. Or, you can create your own.

First, zoom out and ask some questions about the opportunities you're seeking. Write them down and hang next to your desk or in a prominent place where you'll see it every day. Are you looking for gigs, an internship, a job, or to get accepted to a prestigious school? Whether shorter or longer term, keep your goals in front of you at all times. Look at your goals several times a day, while you envision what your life will look like when you achieve them. Writing down your goals and keeping them in front of you is something most successful people do.

Action Steps:

1. Consider your sourcing methods, and how you might meet more people who could help you reach your goals.
2. Consider who's in your network now, and who you'd like to add in the future.
3. Strategize about how to connect with them, whether in person or online.
4. Write your goals on a piece of paper and hang it where you will see it every day.

We are always sourcing. Now, let's look at some great next action steps you should take in your networking game.

Build It, and They Will Come: The Tickler File

Getting organized and implementing a system for following up with new contacts is where many drop the ball, as I've pointed out. It's understandable, since doing this correctly demands special skill, forethought, time, and tenacity.

As you scale your network up from hundreds to thousands, how you manage your contacts gets more important. You need a system to track all your communications. Technology is your friend. The term *Client Relationship Management* (CRM) is often used to describe software systems that help organize and track communications with your network. Some CRM systems allow you to automate functions such as mailing out a newsletter or sending regular updates by e-mail. If you are using social media as part of your strategy, there are some aggregators that allow you to see and manage all your accounts from a simple dashboard.

Before the internet took over our lives, we used something called a "tickler file." This was an expandable cardboard folder with a pocket for each month, and a folder for each week of each month. There were 52 folders for a year. You could still create an old-fashioned tickler file, but it's probably easier to do it on your computer. Here's how this system works.

Action Steps:
When you meet someone for the first time:
1. Write a follow up note to them within 24 to 48 hours, send by mail (or e-mail).
2. Call them on the phone to check in and make sure the channel is open.
3. Make a decision about when you want to contact them next, with a few notes on what you talked about last.
4. Put their card with contact into the tickler file's appropriate week for your next contact.
5. Enter their details into your contacts file (rolodex, database, etc.).

Take all five of these steps very soon after meeting them, preferably within 24 to 48 hours. There's a purpose for each step:

Step 1: Initial Follow-Up

Reaching out to them quickly increases the likelihood they will remember you from your first meeting, and what you talked about. It shows you care about them enough to be proactive about keeping in touch. It sets you apart from others, since most people don't do this. You can really stand out if you send them something by snail mail, since almost no one does this today.

Step 2: Personal Call

A personal call solidifies the impression you made with your initial follow-up. When you call, say you are just checking that the number works, and thank them again for taking the time to speak with you at your first meeting. It's very polite and adds the personal touch of hearing your voice. If you reach their voicemail, leave a short friendly message with your contact number, but don't make it sound like they need to call back. Just say you're checking in to say a friendly hello and that you're still thinking about them and enjoyed your meeting. They should feel a little flattered, and you have nothing to lose except the few minutes it takes to make the call.

Step 3: Decide When to Contact Them Next

Depending on the individual, you might let some time go by before reaching out again. Unless there is some reason to get back in touch sooner, three to six months is fairly standard. Be careful not to seem pushy by calling too frequently. Choose a reasonable time frame, look at the calendar, and make a note of the next time you will contact them. (If a good reason comes up, you can always decide to call them again sooner.) Also make a brief note about what you discussed during your initial conversations, so you can refer to it later on.

Step 4: Put Their Card Into the Correct File

Move their contact to the properly dated folder in the file. This is how the tickler file works; it reminds you who to contact and when to contact them, when the last contact occurred, and what you talked about. That's a lot of information to hold in your head for hundreds or thousands of people. Make sure to look at the file every week so you are reminded of who needs to hear from you that week, or set up automated reminders.

Step 5: Catalogue the New Contact

As a backup, and so you have everyone's contact in one location, enter their name and information into your searchable master database or contacts file (rolodex). This way you can always find their information when needed. Be sure to include a few notes about what they do and how you met. Include the company they work for if appropriate, to make it easier to find them if you forget their name.

The tickler file is the heart and soul of your networking CRM system. Investigate different technologies for solutions that work best. There are some free programs you can use when your network is small, but as it grows you may have to pay for a monthly subscription. MailChimp and Constant Contact are two popular plaforms. Or, you can buy specialized software for the purpose. Continue to organize and leverage your network as it grows. It's a time-consuming process that requires constant attention and persistence, but the results will be worth it.

Give and Take: Relationship Marketing

In his book *Give and Take: A Revolutionary Approach to Success* (Penguin Books, 2013), Wharton psychology professor Adam Grant writes that there are three kinds of people in the world: givers, takers, and transactional. Counterintuitively, the givers are on average more successful in their careers than the other two types (as long as they protect themselves from being taken advantage of by the takers). Grant shows that those who add value to their connections by giving, with no expectation of anything in return, benefit from their network long term by building confidence and trust in their professional relationships.

I call this process *relationship marketing*. Always look for ways to be of service to the people in your network. For example, if you see an article one of your connections would be interested in, forward it to them. If you hear of an opportunity, send it along. Or, have a conversation and listen to them as a way to help them visualize their next steps or solve a problem.

Always start by thinking of how you can help others in your network. Be a friend to gain one. A friendship based on business is better than a business based on a friendship! Making daily small efforts to help others is how you begin to leverage your network. The givers in your network will reciprocate. As Bob Dylan sings: "You gotta *serve* somebody."

Networking Makes the Difference

It's altruistic to help others in your network. Helping others is the goal. Learning about others will make it easier to support them in some way, great or small. But what's in it for us? How does all this help us achieve our goals? If you're in a job search, know that most job opportunities are never advertised. You will hear of them through your network. Freelancers need a steady stream of work. Your clients will find you through your network.

Over time, you will get results from networking by keeping your goals in front of you, tracking your communications, being persistent and tenacious, staying on top of sourcing, and continuing to look for ways to help others as you build your networking skills. Think of it as your opportunity machine.

Heart and Soul of Networking: Authenticity, Integrity, Persistence, and Transparency

The most successful people are almost always active networkers. They know who they are, where they are headed, and they enjoy adding value to others. They have systems for sourcing, maintaining, and leveraging their network to benefit their connections. They are transparent, honest, and eager to engage with other networkers. This is the heart and soul of networking. It works if you work it.

Authenticity means being yourself. People respond to authenticity and quickly notice deception. Integrity means saying what you do and doing what you say. People with integrity are seen as reliable and consistent. When you consistently help others, they will respond and reciprocate. Build trust through reliability and authenticity.

The biggest difference in your life one year from now is likely to come from books you read and people you meet. A single chance meeting can change your career trajectory. Make it your goal to serve others, and follow through at every opportunity. Watch your opportunities multiply and your career flourish.

CHAPTER 10

Seven Steps to the Sale: How to Sell Your Music and Yourself

Sales and selling gets a bad rap. When I ask for word associations with the word salesperson, I often get responses like "sleazy," "pushy," or "liar." I used to think the same way and could never imagine myself selling. Fortunately, I kept an open mind about it. I couldn't have been more wrong.

The true sales pro knows selling is about helping people and teaching them how to get what they want. I use the word "teaching" because people look to salespeople to learn about their options. Sales professionals provide an invaluable service. Every product and service must be sold. To survive as musicians, we must learn to sell. Every sale progresses naturally through seven distinct stages or steps. Once you learn the steps, it becomes easier. Understanding and implementing these steps will transform your life.

Sales Is a Noble Profession

As I learned more about selling, I gained an appreciation for the necessity and importance of sales. Selling well can help you thrive in the music business. Everything has to be sold: The clothes you wear, the chair you sit in, the carpet on the floor, the paint on the wall, the light bulbs and fixtures, the cleaning products in your home, this computer, all of it had to be sold. Allow me to illustrate further.

The U.S. *Gross National Product* (GNP), a measurement in dollars of all goods and services sold annually, has recently been estimated at $20 trillion, excluding housing. Consumer spending accounts for roughly two-thirds of that amount. The markup (margin or profit) on sales of goods and services can vary from a few percent to 50 percent, 60 percent, or even as high as 90 percent. Whatever the percentage, there's a lot of money changing hands in the economy, and salespeople are getting paid quite nicely to help customers get what they want.

The Job of the Salesperson

When I ask my students what is the job of a salesperson, they usually respond with answers, such as: "to sell stuff" or "make people buy things." A common misperception about selling is that the job of a salesperson is to move inventory and get people to buy stuff. Success is measured that way, so it's understandable that people believe it. However, getting people to buy has little to do with what the salesperson really does.

More accurately, a salesperson *helps people get what they want.* In order to get what they want, people need information. By knowing all about their product or service (including the competition) and sharing that information freely, a salesperson helps the customer decide. Knowing how to sell holds the key to the lifestyle you want.

As with music, or networking, some have a natural talent for sales. For the rest of us, a little training goes a long way. Set the goal of improving your ability at sales, and make a habit of measuring your progress. The seven steps will help you do this.

How to Use the Seven Steps

Awareness of these steps can guide you and increase your chances for success. You can't win them all, but awareness of the steps to the sale can help you win more often and benefit more from your sales.

A core principle is to always maintain *control,* to be able to help your customer by guiding the process. If you let your prospect control you, you can't serve them properly. Learn how to maintain control, for example, by slowing things down. Use psychology to help you. Using key words and phrases, moderating your voice, and using body language (if not on the phone) can help you control the process.

The time spent on each step will vary. Things can move very quickly, or they can take a while. Keep careful notes as you go; this is very import-ant. Keep careful track of the sales process. Be aware of what is going on around you. Learn from your mistakes, so as not to repeat them. The more you practice, the better you will get. Don't jump around in the steps. Remember, your job is to help your client get what they want. When you stick to the steps in order, both you and your client stand to gain.

The steps are very logical and easy to understand. The process is simple, but that doesn't mean it's easy. These steps apply universally, no matter what you are selling.

Step One: Meet and Greet

The cliché rings true: You have only one chance to make a first impression. You can make it or break it at the beginning. All business is personal, since people want to buy from someone they trust. The initial meeting is where you size each other up to see if there's a chance to build trust. Your prospect wants to know that if there's a problem, you will make it right. How you greet someone influences their opinion of your trustworthiness. It should not be taken lightly.

It takes less than one minute for a prospect to decide if they like you and to decide whether or not they think they can trust you. It's crucial to be your natural self. Don't pretend to be someone or something you're not. Be confident, offer a firm dry handshake (don't break their fingers though), and look them straight in the eye. If you are answering the phone, give your name. Use your tone of voice and posture to show that you are here to help. Ask their name and write it down. Confirm the spelling and get their contact, so you can follow up. Taking notes keeps you from having to ask them the same question twice, shows you're paying close attention, and demonstrates you are serious about helping them.

Action Steps for sales by phone:
1. Use proper phone etiquette.
2. Choose a quiet place for the call and be unhurried in your conversation. If it's not a good time to talk, say so, get their number, and set up a time to call back. If you use voicemail, remember that people are busy and keep your greeting and instructions as brief as possible.
3. Smile when you talk on the phone, as this comes across in the tone of your voice.

4. Don't pace the room while you are talking.
5. Do take notes when on the phone. This means you shouldn't talk while you are driving.

To summarize, in the first step we greet our prospect in a sincere and personal manner, offer our name and get theirs, thank them for considering us, and establish that we are there to help. This builds trust, shows professionalism, sets the pace, puts them at ease, and allows you to take control of the sale.

Step Two: Qualify, Ask Questions, Listen to the Answers

In this second step, the goal is to find out what the prospect wants and if you can help them get it. This is called "qualifying" in the sales world and helps you understand if they are a good fit. A good fit can mean that they have a job you want to do, they can pay you, and they won't have a difficult personality. For example, you and your band may not want to play certain types of events that don't align with your values or an organization may want you to play for free or at a very low price. Asking the right questions will help you get answers.

You will need to ask questions and listen carefully to their answers. People don't always say what they mean, and just because you are honest doesn't mean they are honest, clear or accurate. They might not yet know what they want, or can afford, and your job is to help them wherever they are in the process. Write down what they say, so you can review it later. Have a list of what to ask, so you don't forget important questions. Asking the right questions to properly *qualify* your prospect can be half the battle.

As you listen, try to grasp their true motives and desires. For example, people don't buy cars just for transportation. They may have several cars already. People buy cars for status, convenience, luxury, or fulfillment of a dream. With music, people don't only hire a band to play music. They will have other reasons. For example, a club owner hires a band to attract customers, keep them on premises, and sell food and drinks. Someone planning a quiet dinner hires musicians to provide ambience, and mask light conversation in the room. Someone planning a raucous party or wedding celebration will book a dance/party band to get their guests out on the dance floor and keep them there. Sometimes the goal is to raise money for a cause. There are even times when neighbors try to outdo each other as with landscaping or spending lavishly on home decorating! Who can hire the better band and throw the best party?

Listen for the real reasons people want to buy, so you can address their real needs and wants. This understanding will guide you through the following steps, so get the information early on. Stay in control of the sale, and don't let them ask all the questions, so you can find out what you need to know in order to really help them.

Estimate Versus Quote

What if a client asks your price before you qualify them? You can't quote them a price without knowing what they want. You can give them an estimate. An *estimate* is different from a quote in two ways: It's a range between two numbers, and most importantly, you aren't bound by it. You must always honor any *quote* you give. An estimate is just your best guess at this moment what the final price range might be, based on the information you have. You can always adjust it later, as you get more information.

Watch out for the client who is pushy and just asking about the fee. They are trying to control the sale, which makes it harder for you to do your job. If a prospect treats you rudely, seems impatient, and pushes you around, they are more likely to act unreasonably later on. Experience taught me this type of client will be demanding and troublesome, and is more trouble than they are worth. Not all money is good money, and sometimes it's just better to walk away. Setting up a proper negotiation requires artistry, and we'll return to estimates and quotes in step four.

When you can't provide what the client wants, it's smart to refer them to someone else who can help them, even if it's a competitor, because they'll remember you had their interests in mind. They could come back when they need what you offer and will usually tell others about you. As a customer, it's frustrating when you can't find what you need. Always try to help the customer, as it builds goodwill that leads to sales later on. Giving a referral is just another way to help them, if you don't offer what they are looking for.

Step Three: Sell Value, Not Price

Now that you know what your prospect wants, and think you can help, it's time to sell the value of your service or product. For this, you need detailed knowledge of your product or service and how it will help the customer. Remember, your customer often wants the benefit and not just the product or service itself. If you've done step two properly, you will be attuned to their real needs and wants.

To put your prospect at ease and sell value, talk about your other satisfied customers. Knowing that others have bought is comforting to a buyer. That's why you see ads saying "number 1 selling brand." For example, if a client wants to hire your band for a wedding, talk about other weddings you've done that were similar. You can offer to have them talk to previous clients about you (be certain to get permission first), and it's also smart to have some written or video testimonials.

Avoid using the price as a selling point, unless budget is a major concern. Clients are suspicious of a low price, thinking to themselves "What am I not getting?" There is no such thing as a free lunch, as the expression goes. Clients are especially suspicious of the word *free*. (Aren't you?) People expect to pay for what they get and hope to get what they pay for. There's a difference. Asking a price that's fair gives them confidence in you as a professional and allows you to eat. Price signals value. Selling on the basis of a lower price alone isn't a reliable strategy. Let them pay a fair price. They expect to.

When selling value, never speak negatively about a competitor. Trashing the competition will make you look bad. Your client may disagree with you and you will have maligned their taste and judgment. (There's no accounting for taste.) Know what the competition offers and how to differentiate yourself from them. This was in your business plan and should be backed up by your marketing materials. Talk about what makes you different, the value of your offering, and stress the benefits they will get from buying. This differentiator is called your *unique selling point* (USP).

Action Steps:
1. Talk about other satisfied customers to put your prospect at ease.
2. Get testimonials from past clients.
3. Focus on the value you bring and avoid using price as the selling point.

4. Never speak negatively about the competition. In case you are asked, have honest points about how your business is different and describe that without saying anything negative about your competition.
5. Prepare these items in advance of your phone call or meeting.

Step Four: Negotiation

This is the middle step, and the heart of selling. Volumes have been written about negotiating. There're case studies and books to help you improve at this ancient practice. Colleges and business schools offer courses and even degrees in negotiating. Psychology and culture play a role in how people negotiate business deals. In a sense, we must negotiate for everything we want in life, not just in business. Negotiating is as old as humankind itself.

Those who lack experience negotiating can feel intimidated by it. They fear they stand to lose if they negotiate poorly, and they could be right. The confrontational nature is a turn-off, and they might have been previously victimized by self-dealing salespeople. However, without a proper negotiation, many transactions cannot happen. Negotiations exist to ensure that each party can get the best deal possible. We negotiate to learn what's possible and to determine fair price, sometimes called *price discovery* in economics, because negotiated sales are the best indicator of true value.

If you have qualified your prospect, and sold your value, you should have what you need to begin a negotiation. A professional negotiator stays in control and has tools for handling a negotiation smoothly and effectively. Once you get past the fear, negotiating can actually be fun! Negotiating presents challenges to the best salespeople, and believe me when I tell you that they do enjoy it, even when it gets hard. The more you do it, the more natural it becomes. Fear is the biggest enemy, so just get over that as quickly as possible, and accept that a negotiation will have to happen for you and the client to get what you both want. Think of it as a game.

How to Negotiate: Overcome Obstacles

In literature on sales and selling, you will read that *obstacles are opportunities.* At first, I didn't relate to this, but through experience I came to understand it better. If your customer has an objection, it's your job to help them overcome it. It's about helping them. What is keeping them from making a deal right now? If you can find the obstacles and remove them, you can get to the next step. Here's how it works.

You need three pieces of information. The first is the lowest amount you can accept. I call this a *cutoff*, and it's like a floor. If you can't get this lowest possible price, you should leave the negotiation. They can always come back later with a better offer. Some things are not worth doing for too little. You shouldn't give anything away out of desperation to make a sale. You also have costs and could lose money if you don't establish your price floor.

The second number you need is your *anchor*, or asking price. It's like the sticker price on a car. People know they can usually negotiate a better price. Choosing the anchor price is important because you need to leave room to lower it if your client objects. Research shows that the higher the anchor, the higher the final selling price, but this only works to a point. If your anchor is too high, the client could balk. Your anchor is the Goldilocks number: not too high or too low, but just right. It's your claim to value.

The third number you should have in your head is what you actually expect to get. It's your *realistic* number and you hope to get there. It's somewhere in between the other two. How much should you ask for? The rule is to always ask for more than you think you can get. You need to get the most you can, while still maintaining competitiveness in the market and serving the client. As you make concessions, you should ask your client to also make concessions in the name of fairness.

When it's time to quote your asking price, state your price first and wait for a response from the buyer. If the buyer objects to the price, you can lower your price, and overcome the objection. This is why objections are opportunities—after all, they are not objecting to you, only your price. You *want* them to object to your price. If they don't, you'll wonder if your price was too low. At the same time, never overcharge the client. There's a balance here. You never get money for nothing, and in the end you want happy customers. The price should be high enough to surprise them, but not so high as to seem unrealistic in light of the value of your service.

Negotiations can get bogged down for any number of reasons. You might need to return to selling value in step three, or qualifying in step two, by asking more questions. If I've met their price demands and they still can't decide, maybe they aren't ready to buy. It comes down to their *desire, need,* and *ability* to buy (DNA). This isn't only about money. You want to do a great job and please your clients. Happy customers bring more customers. There are costs to doing business, and everyone has bills to pay.

Negotiating is not a zero-sum game where the winner takes all. It's more like a cooperative exchange where everyone wins. Rudeness, deceit, and dishonesty have no place in negotiations, as the goal is to come to an agreement. It's a potential win–win situation. And there are certainly times when it is better not to make a deal.

Step Five: Closing

Step five is the *closing.* After your successful negotiation, you must write a contract and get a deposit. In order for a closing to occur, money has to change hands. This is a show of goodwill on the part of the client and validates the contract in the eyes of the law. Just as there's no standard fee, there is no standard deposit. It could be 5 percent, 10 percent, 50 percent, or even payment in full. It's whatever you and your client agree upon. They will give you some money as a down payment to show they intend to honor your deal. This is sometimes called *earnest money.*

Their deposit is not your money to keep or spend until after you've delivered your product or service as promised. There's no such thing as a nonrefundable deposit. For legitimate reasons, the client could come back in a day, a week, or a month and cancel the deal. The deposit is simply a sign of good faith. It isn't your money until you've earned it by delivering your product or service. Under certain circumstances, written in the contract, if they cancel, you could keep the deposit as liquidated damages. We will cover live venue performance contracts in the next chapter.

Closing the deal requires that you write a comprehensive contract, with attached rider if needed, that clearly reflects the terms of your agreement. After both parties sign, collect a deposit from your client. Keep deposits in a separate (interest bearing) bank account, and don't touch the money until after the gig.

Step Six: Delivery

Integrity means doing what you say you will do. You must now deliver your service or product. Strive to exceed your client's expectations. Happy customers are the best way to get referrals for future work.

Action Steps:
1. Show up on time and start on time;
2. Dress appropriately, have the right number of musicians;
3. Play the right songs, entertain the crowd or make them dance, mix the sound professionally, and play at a good volume;
4. Be polite and respectful toward guests, your client, the venue staff, and other vendors;
5. Don't take long breaks;
6. End your performance on time;
7. Smile

These are the basics.

At the end of the night, people should be asking for your business cards. Word gets out that you're a good band and easy to work with. You get calls for more gigs. You might get a gratuity from your client (this should always be shared with all the musicians). A delivery that exceeds your client's expectations is the best formula for success.

Step Seven: Follow Up

Do not overlook this last step, as so many people do. Send your client a thank you card. Alternatively, you could call or e-mail. Thank them for their business. Make it personal. Ask for future business and referrals. This is your chance to turn one sale into many.

Your past clients will assume things. They may think you have all the work you need. Ask them to refer you to other prospective clients. Buy a box of thank you cards (it's a tax deductible expense), and write every client a handwritten note the day after the gig. Thank them for the opportunity to perform, make positive comments about the event, and ask them to think of you for future gigs, and to tell their friends about you. It's a great strategy to get more gigs and also common courtesy.

Use satisfied clients as references for prospective clients. Ask their permission first; it's polite and it will remind them to send you referrals. In the lexicon of sales and selling, a *bird dog* is a client who goes out of their way to get work for you because they love what you do. They will tell everyone in their network how great you are and suggest they hire you. If you ever are lucky enough to have such a client, be sure to encourage them. Send them flowers or a gift certificate to a nice restaurant as thanks. They are worth investing in. You can also offer a *finder's fee* to any venue managers or other vendors who are complimentary of your work.

Closing Ratio

You can't win them all, nobody can. You win some, and you lose some. Your *closing ratio* is simply your number of prospects versus your number of sales, expressed as a percentage. It lets you measure how well you're doing over time. For example, if you have 100 inquiries and book 50 gigs, your closing ratio is 50 percent. Since the volume of inquiries will vary, closing ratio is a simple metric to keep track of how well you are closing deals. Log all your inquiries and see if you can improve your ratio over time.

The seven steps progress logically for every sale. Awareness of the steps will help you succeed with your music. Through the steps, you will increase your confidence level, no matter your experience. Sales and selling, done right, will let you prosper.

CHAPTER 11

Get Paid for Your Music, Live Venue Performance Contracts

If you're getting paying gigs or planning to tour with your band, you'll need to have your own live venue *performance contract*. Longer term agreements like recording, production, or management contracts should always be reviewed by your attorney, but a contract for one performance is a fairly simple document you can execute on your own. Arm yourself with some knowledge, pay attention to the details, and your performing experience will be more professional and rewarding.

Make a Deal, Put It in Writing

Having your own well-written contract earns you respect from venue managers and concert promoters. While verbal agreements can be legally binding (it helps if you have witnesses), the gold standard for contracts is the written agreement. It will make everyone's life easier in the event any misunderstandings or disagreements arise.

Human memory is far from infallible. I'll never forget the time I showed up with my band on a Saturday evening to find an irate club-owner, furious because we were not there the previous night. I had clear memories of multiple phone calls about Saturday, but he was certain it was for Friday. Needless to say, we never played there again. This pain could've been avoided with a written contract.

Although an e-mail could be enough to confirm the terms of an agreement, it can be hard to prove where the e-mail originated and that it wasn't doctored. A date-stamped e-mail is certainly better than nothing, but in cases of serious disagreement or accusation of malicious intent, a signed contract will work better. Otherwise, you might need to rely on a sworn affidavit from the sender or recipient which could be time consuming and may not survive close scrutiny.

In short, a written signed contract protects both parties. You might need to explain this to a client who questions whether a contract is needed. Understand how each clause of your contract protects the interests of each party. A good contract protects both sides.

I recommend you never perform without a written contract agreement. Even if there is no money involved, you should create a written "confirmation" where all details and expectations are laid out clearly. It's the safest and most businesslike way.

Boilerplate, What?

Some contract terminology will be the same in every live venue contract. Lawyers call this consistent terminology *boilerplate*. According to an online legal dictionary, boilerplate is: "...slang for provisions in a contract, which are apparently routine and often preprinted. The term comes from an old method of printing. Today boilerplate is commonly stored in computer memory to be retrieved and copied when needed."

Boilerplate is like a template. For example, the very first paragraph usually mentions the parties to the contract and the date the contract is made. Every live venue contract has similar clauses including performance date, times, compensation, and location. Once you've written your performance contract, you won't need to rewrite all of it every time. You can just change names, date, location, and fee amount.

Agreements in Terms Worth Knowing

Now that we understand why we need written contracts, which terms and clauses should we include? To start, consider the following:

- Who are the parties to the agreement (purchaser and artist)?
- When is the agreement made (date)?
- What is the performance date and time?
- Where will the performance take place (address)?
- How many musicians are performing?
- What style of music will be performed on which instruments?

- Compensation—How much will you be paid (deposit and remainder), who should payments be made out to, when are the payments due, and what is the method of payment?
- Is there a possibility of cancellation and/or "rain date"?
- Act of God clause (a.k.a. force majeure)?
- Equipment and/or food, lodging, transportation rider(s)?
- What is the legal jurisdiction of the contract?
- Self-employment/independent contractor clause.
- Attire, other requirements.

You can include asking these questions as part of your client onboarding process, so these important points are clarified early on.

Some of these can be combined in a clause. Before you write the contract, consult your notes from the negotiation, as we discussed in Chapter 10. Let's now have a look at some common live venue contract clauses.

Who, Where, and When?

The very first paragraph states who the parties to the contract are. Use the terms *artist* and *purchaser* to refer to each. For a contract to be considered legally valid, you need the physical address and contact information for both parties.

Be as specific as you can, and follow the agreed times as closely as possible. Above all, never ever start late, as this could invalidate the entire contract.

Plan to end at the time stated in the contract, regardless of any delay in the start time. It's not fair to the musicians to ask them to work longer than the contract end time (without overtime pay) if the delay was not their fault. Musicians may need to leave immediately after a gig to get to another gig. In this case, overtime may not be possible. The client should understand this, too. Interestingly, nothing in the contract stipulates we must play well, but it does say when our performance must begin and end!

Action Steps:
1. In the opening paragraph, include the date the contract is created, with names of artist and purchaser.

2. Put the names and addresses underneath the signatures of each party at the bottom of the contract, including contact info.

3. Next, arrange the clauses after the first paragraph logically, so the contract is easy to read.

4. Create a clause *Date and Times* which lists the exact date of the performance, plus start and end times. If there are scheduled breaks or set lengths, these could also be included here. If there are sound check, load-in, or set up times, specify these too.

5. Include a clause which lists the exact location of the performance. If there's a street address, include it. Add your on-site contact name and their cell phone number, if possible, so you can call if you have trouble finding the venue or stage. If there is a specific room or stage where you must report to, include that information as well.

What, Why, and How Much?

Now that we have the parties to the contracts, and the day, time, and place, we may wish to include some more details about the performance.

Action Steps:
Decide if you need to include a clause called Special Conditions, which will address:

1. The number of musicians;
2. What style of music is to be played and on what instruments;
3. How the musicians will be attired;
4. Who is responsible for music directing or other roles, for example, master of ceremonies (MC);
5. Dressing rooms;
6. Meals or refreshments for musicians;
7. What type of event or production the music is supporting, for example, fund-raiser, wedding, political rally, or festival.

Note that some of these items may also be included in an attached rider. The *rider* is an additional page or pages attached to the contract outlining all requirements too detailed or lengthy to be included in the main contract, such as travel arrangements, equipment needs (may also be in a separate equipment rider), and food and lodging. Note that if a rider is attached to a contract, the contract needs a clause in it stating that the rider is attached and how many pages it comprises.

This brings us to a clause of great interest: compensation. This can be broken out as follows:

- *Total compensation* (can also be called *performance fee* or similar)
- *Deposit* and *remainder* (in some cases multiple remainder payments)
- *Method of payment* and to whom
- Due dates for deposit and remainder(s)

Note that the deposit and remainder(s) should add up to the total compensation or performance fee. In cases where *invoicing* (billing) the client or employer is required, the compensation clause in the contract becomes a guide to creating the invoices. On each invoice you will need to include what the payment is for, when it is due, and to whom it should be paid. In general, you need to prepare invoices when the purchaser is a company or organization, as they will require them for their internal accounting procedures. Private individuals do not usually require an invoice.

What Else Do We Need?

Other considerations exist beyond the who, what, where, why, when, and how much. A clause may be included that spells out what happens if either party needs to cancel. Typically, there is a time period, often 30 to 60 days from the performance date where the contract can be cancelled without penalty. In this case, you might need to return the deposit. That's why it is important that you don't spend the deposit before doing the gig. I've seen some people get into trouble this way.

If the gig is outdoors, you might also have a provision for inclement weather. This is called a *rain date* but weather-related reasons for moving the performance date are not limited to only rain. Poor ticket sales could lead to cancellation. In a case where a gig was cancelled at the last minute, with possible malicious intent, (for example, they hired a different band), you may be entitled to keep the deposit as liquidated damages and pursue them for the remainder. You don't need a lawyer for this in most cases, as you can use *small claims court* for lesser amounts. In Massachusetts, where I live, the limit is $7,000 for small claims.

I try to limit my live venue contract to a single page. If there are many specific details related to travel, equipment, lodging, meals, and so on, it may make sense to add a rider to the contract. As mentioned earlier, it's crucial to list the number of pages in the rider on the contract.

No Brown M&Ms, Please

Most musicians have heard the story about Eddie Van Halen's tour rider demanding a bowl of M&Ms with all the brown ones taken out. The story took on the status of urban legend symbolizing the excesses of some rock stars' frivolous contractual demands. According to the myth-debunking site Snopes:

> The legendary "no brown M&Ms" contract clause was indeed real, but the purported motivation for it was not. The M&Ms provision was included in Van Halen's contracts not as an act of caprice, but because it served a practical purpose: to provide a simple way of determining whether the technical specifications of the contract had been thoroughly read and complied with.

(As told by Van Halen lead singer David Lee Roth in his autobiography.) So, apparently, this was a true story.

Who's the Boss? Depends…

Three final potential clauses are worthy of mention: the *self-employment clause* (sometimes called *independent contractor*), the *force majeure*, and the *jurisdiction clause*.

The self-employment clause states that the contract does not create an employer–employee relationship, and that the performer or band is an independent contractor. Remember I wrote earlier that the contract should protect the interest of both parties? In this case, the clause protects an employer from liability for payroll tax withholding, unemployment insurance, retirement and health benefits, or other benefits usually offered to regular employees, and as required by law. From the perspective of the artist, being a nonemployee establishes certain rights of control, for example, over songs to be played, or set order.

Force majeure, also called *Act of God* clause, protects both parties from liability if there is some unforeseen event that precludes the performance taking place. Examples might include snowstorms, earthquakes, pandemics, floods, riots, wars, car accidents, terrorist attacks, or illnesses. Anything that could disrupt the performance and is clearly beyond anyone's control could fall into this category. The force majeure clause states that neither party can be held accountable for such events.

Finally, the jurisdiction clause simply states which laws will apply to the agreement. In most cases, the laws of the state where the performance is to take place will prevail. If both parties are from a different state than the location of the gig, then the state where you live would be the best, although it could also be the state of the counterparty. As with almost everything in the contract, the jurisdiction may be negotiable.

Sign on the Dotted Line

Now that all the t's are crossed and the i's are dotted, all that's left is to sign and date the contracts above the printed name and address of both parties.

Make sure you have a physical address for both parties, as the contract may be invalid or unenforceable without it (a P.O. box won't do). If you aren't in the same room, the procedure for signing is to send two copies of the contract out unsigned, for the client to review. Sometimes they will write in changes, or cross something out, which is why you should only sign it after they return the copies with their signature affixed and the required deposit. Otherwise, your signature might end up below something you didn't agree to. In most cases, receipt of the deposit along with the signed contract will mean that the contract is in effect. If you are using a digital contract, be sure they sign it first.

If you are writing your first contract, you might want to ask another more established musician to show you theirs.

Pro Tip:
Always remember that a contract is only as good as the word of the two parties in the agreement. Contracts are not always adhered to, so don't be surprised if someone breaks a contract or doesn't live up to their obligations. It's a good idea to check up on the background and reputation of the other party before entering into a contract, so you will know what to expect.

CHAPTER 12

Industry Trends, Starting and Growing Your Business as an Entrepreneur

I was driving in my car one night, listening to an interview with a successful serial entrepreneur on Bloomberg News. The interviewer asked what seemed like a simple question: What was the most difficult part of launching this new business?

The entrepreneur paused for a moment and answered the question with one word: everything. She went on to describe various aspects of the preparation and launch, and how nothing was ever easy or went smoothly. Her answer epitomized the challenges faced by any budding entrepreneur. Nothing about business is ever easy. Hey, if it was easy, everyone would be doing it!

The fact that it's difficult doesn't discourage the entrepreneur, because they're attracted to doing hard things. The rewards are high in the winner-take-all cutthroat world of business. Even if you're wildly successful, this will encourage competitors to come into the market. Getting to the top is one thing, staying there is a whole different game. In this chapter I'll highlight some challenges and opportunities every business owner will likely face in meeting current and future trends.

Your Mission: Look Around Corners to Anticipate Industry Changes

To succeed in starting your music business, and to stay successful, you'll need to constantly be on the lookout for changes in our industry and in your market. It's crucial to follow the news, read books to increase your knowledge, and have sensitive feelers out so you are prepared for the inevitable change. While there are countless uncertainties, and no one knows what the future will hold, we do know the only constant is change.

To stay on top of a rapidly changing business landscape, there are times when you should play offense, and other times you should act defensively. The entrepreneur must do their best to look around corners to anticipate the coming changes and to be ready for those new developments. Some entrepreneurs seem to have a special kind of vision that allows them to do this.

Knowing the road ahead can give an incredible advantage in business. The winds of change can shift at any time, and businesses must stay agile to survive. This could mean many things, from constantly putting out new music, choosing the right marketing channels, and adopting new technology, to changing how you interact with clients, customers, and partners to develop and grow new revenue streams. The larger an organization gets, the harder it will become to do these things. Once you have launched your music business, to continue to thrive, you should look for ways to expand the business and grow your revenues, while anticipating and managing change.

Following are some current trends that impact the music industry, and will likely continue to do so.

- Streaming (music and video)
- Social and business platforms
- Cobranding
- Music aggregators
- Geofencing, e-Commerce, AI-AR-VR, holograms, and robotics
- Search, SEO, SEM
- Vinyl, CDs, analogue tape, and downloads
- Technology and music production
- Music services
- Horizontal versus vertical expansion
- CRM platforms
- Blockchain technology and cryptocurrencies

Action Step:
As you consider each of these trends, imagine how they might impact or interact with your own business idea.

Streaming

The biggest change in the music industry over the last decade has been the mainstream adoption of streaming music and video as the primary means of consumption. For recorded music, the progression from physical products (vinyl, cassette, compact disc) to digital, which started with file sharing in the 1990s, and then downloads, seems complete. iTunes has stopped offering paid downloads, and subscription services like Spotify and Tidal now rule the day. This has negatively impacted the bottom line for artists, record companies, and publishers, as streaming pays much less than previous sales of physical copies and downloads did.

New legislation such as the Music Modernization Act of 2018 (MMA) has attempted to protect artists and producers from losing their livelihoods, but the fact is that revenues from recorded music have fallen precipitously over the last two decades. This means the revenue pie has gotten much smaller. We'll take a closer look at music streaming in the next chapter.

Social and Business Platforms

Music artists have adopted social media platforms to promote their music, putting traditional music publicists out of business. There's a new job title in the industry: *social media manager*. Many artists choose to do it themselves, either to save money or because they prefer to connect directly with their fans. Effective use of social media has become an indispensable skill for artists.

With the rise of social media over the years, the landscape appears to be flattened so anyone can break through to fame and fortune by putting out quality content on sites such as Instagram, SoundCloud, Twitter, Facebook, YouTube, and TikTok. This is true to an extent. Because of this, more people are trying to do just that, making it even tougher for new artists to cut through all the noise.

Since earning any real money from streaming recordings is difficult, many artists became resigned to giving their music away for free or allowing fans to pay whatever they wish, sometimes through crowdfunding sites. Artists have looked for other ways to earn money, such as through live performances, or by offering other services and products. Most artists give concerts and sell branded merchandise to make ends meet.

Artists have always found a way to survive, and will continue to do so. Effective use of social media platforms has been a boon for the self-promoting musician, and can open doors to other earning opportunities. Business platforms like LinkedIn, Wix, Squarespace, Bandzoogle, and Patreon offer more ways to promote your music and to connect with fans and other businesses.

Cobranding

Many artists seek to cobrand with other companies, using their image and music to sell products and services from which they receive a portion of the revenues. For example, having a clothing line, cosmetics, perfume, alcoholic beverages, or even tourist excursions in the market has become *de rigueur* for artists. Examples abound, especially in pop music; it almost seems that everyone is using their image to sell something besides music.

People seek to enhance their self-image through association with brands. This is a well-known tenet in the psychology of marketing. From the artists' perspective, if they love my music, they might love other products associated with my brand. Just like sports figures are paid huge sums for endorsements of products, musicians can harness the power of their image in order to earn huge sums of money.

Music Aggregators

Music aggregators have become more and more important to artists seeking to get their music out through all channels: social media, streaming, physical sales, licensing, and syndication. Aggregator sites allow musicians to distribute their music globally through online stores and streaming platforms, usually charging an up-front fee or sharing in the revenues from sales and licensing of music. They also help musicians manage their websites, ticket sales, merchandise, fan clubs, newsletters, and tour calendars.

Aggregators such as Bandzoogle, TuneCore, CD Baby, DistroKid, BandCamp, and SonicBids have carved out an important niche in the music industry. The competition is fierce, keeping the cost to musicians relatively low. Most artists now use some sort of aggregator for managing their music business. Choosing the right one is a matter of identifying and comparing the different ones to see which works best for your own situation.

GeoFencing, VR, AI, e-Commerce, and Holograms

Imagine you bought a ticket to see your favorite artist and are driving to the concert hall in a neighboring city or town. The artist has set up a *geofence* with a one mile perimeter around the venue. A geofence uses triangulated cell tower technology to know when you, the ticket holder, have crossed the perimeter. Once you do, you receive a push message through your smartphone app telling you to reserve your parking space at the venue, with a substantial discount. Of course, you do it, and enter the garage showing your phone at the entrance, secure in the knowledge that your spot is reserved and already paid for. At the end of the night, you can just drive out, without worrying about waiting in line to pay for your parking.

Next, as you walk from the garage to the venue, you get another message telling you that the concert doesn't begin for another 45 minutes, and the pizza shop across the street will give you a free pitcher of beer with your order of a large pizza, which is already cooked and waiting for you. You are hungry and thirsty, don't know what else is going to be available to eat and drink inside the concert, so you go feed your face and drink the free beer. No need to ask for the check, or leave a tip, it's all been handled on your smartphone.

During the concert, you select and pay for your merchandise on your phone, which gets handed to you as you leave the hall. This is not the future I am writing about here. Technology makes this possible, today, and everything we need to do this has already been available for some time. I should mention that the artist receives a percentage of all revenue their fans spend on parking and food on the way to their concert. After all, they are coming to see you, so why shouldn't the local vendors be willing to give up some of their revenue for the extra business? The money they keep is money they wouldn't have had otherwise.

This story gets even better. Since the artist now has access to you via the app on your phone, they know what town you live in. They might be able to use that information to help book a show in your town and can then advertise the show directly to you and other fans via the phone. There are people who might opt out of this scheme for privacy reasons, but your die-hard fans will be happy to be connected this way, and hear directly from you about upcoming shows. e-Commerce, AI-AR-VR, holograms, robotics, and geofencing, as I've just described, are not the only futuristic technologies artists can use to enhance the fan experience. Combined with *artificial intelligence* (AI) and big data mining, a computer algorithm can learn all about your buying behaviors, with the goals of predicting exactly what you will want next, and putting it in front of you at the exact moment you want to buy it. Combined with other technology, like geofencing, social media analytics, and search engines, AI can become a powerful e-commerce tool.

AI and *augmented reality* (AR), along with *virtual reality* (VR), are all becoming important weapons in the artist's arsenal for delivering a unique compelling entertainment experience. Algorithms determine the playlist of songs you listen to on your streaming platform. They can choose the next song based on your mood, time of day, the weather, or your location.

Wearing a headset, you might be able to watch a music video in 3D, or integrate your own sense of reality into the video by moving your head, your eyes, or other body parts. Your music might be integrated into your favorite video game. You can immerse yourself in different experiences, changing your perspective at will. For example, maybe you'd like to watch your favorite concert video from behind the artist on stage. Or conduct the orchestra.

Once you add *holograms* into this picture, it really starts to get intriguing. Imagine being on stage in New York and having people watching you in a theater in Tokyo. This is now possible, although the technology to make it happen is still quite expensive. There have been some shows that used holograms of deceased performers, mixing them on stage with real live performers. From the audience perspective, it's hard to tell which performer is real.

The Japanese seem to have taken the lead with building humanoid robots. There are now extremely lifelike robots that can give lectures to students in a lecture hall, while being simultaneously controlled from a remote location. With this emerging technology, it really is possible to be in more than one place at the same time.

Search, SEO, SEM

Search engines on the Web have become more important for promotion, marketing, and all kinds of research. In the west, Google is the predominant search engine, yet others such as Bing and Yahoo have remained relevant. In Asia and other parts of the world, different search engines are in use, like Baidu in China.

Search Engine Optimization (SEO) is the practice of using various tactics (coding, content, website structure enhancements) to attract website visitors. Part of that includes purposefully creating useful content on the web to achieve organic reach, meaning that the content will show up in searches using specific keywords. Creating content specifically to appear in searches conducted by people in search engines has become a specialty in marketing and computer coding. Not all musicians and artists are up to speed on SEO, I've found, but marketing people certainly are, because it's a crucial technique to understand and employ for anyone in business today.

Using the *Google Ads Keyword Research Tool*, or another keyword planner, for example, one can see exactly how many times a given term has been used in a search over a set time and in which specific geographical locations. One can also see how competitive search keywords are, based on the percentage of advertisers who are using them in paid advertisements online. The purpose of SEO is to get your content or website in front of people when they are searching for something you offer in your business.

For example, if you are offering guitar lessons, you could use the keyword research tool to determine which phrases people enter when looking for lessons. You might find that they use the phrase *guitar instruction* far less than *how to play guitar*. In this case, you should create your content using the latter phrase if you wish to appear in more search results from prospective students in your area.

The prior example illustrates the mechanism of organic reach by using SEO. The aim of the search engine is to return the most useful and appropriate content in search results, so it will help you to appear in search results for prospective customers if you are creating useful and relevant content for the various queries they use.

Action Steps:
1. Search your favorite search engine for a keyword planner tool.
2. Try one or two keywords out, and analyze search terms you can find related to what you do.
3. Check the search results of your keywords to see what information is offered as useful to searchers.

Search Engine Marketing (SEM) is a broader technique that includes SEO, but incorporates paid advertising or *pay per click* (PPC) techniques. For example, if you are a blues player giving a concert in Minneapolis, you could pay Google to have your ad pop up on the side of the page when someone is watching a blues artist on YouTube when in Minneapolis (YouTube is owned by Google).

SEO and SEM are forms of *inbound marketing,* meaning the advertiser is trying to get their content in front of a prospect at the moment they are looking to buy something online. It's different from *outbound marketing,* which is what we normally think of as traditional advertising, for example, television ads, billboards, magazine ads, and any other type of advertising that broadcasts messages out for all to see and hear.

Action Step:
Decide if you want SEO and/or PPC ads to be part of your marketing.

Vinyl, CDs, Analogue Tape, and Downloads

Let's go back to the future for a moment, and consider that what goes around, comes around. A hit song from 20 years ago can make a return to the hit parade with a fresh version. In the same way, older technologies seem to never die, and may even have a resurgence in popularity. Although *vinyl records* (LPs, EPs, and 45s) faded from the mainstream decades ago after the introduction of *the compact disc* (CD), there are still die-hard vinyl fans and collectors, and some independent artists still release new music on vinyl, whether exclusively or as limited editions. Highly collectable vinyl records can fetch large sums of money. There are still music stores selling vinyl records, and the manufacturers of vinyl records are stretched to capacity.

Analogue recording studios haven't disappeared, either. Many musicians and engineers swear by the warmth and fullness of analogue recordings, compared to digital recordings, which can sound harsh and cold. They create all their recordings in a studio using technology from 50 years ago, and at the very end convert it to the digital format for mastering, distribution, and sale. This isn't unusual and highlights that there will always be a niche market for past styles of music and technology. CDs are nowadays used by musicians as calling cards, either given away for free or sold at concerts and clubs. Some musicians have started offering their music on credit card-sized USBs that fit in your wallet and plug easily into a laptop computer or smartphone.

Downloads haven't disappeared. Many people prefer to have their music in the form of a *downloadable file* (MP3) so they can listen while not connected to the internet. Downloads work well for networked services, for example, where many devices are connected to a central computer allowing music to be played remotely without internet access. Everything old can be new again.

Technology and Music Production

Of course music technology has come a long way since the days of analogue recording. Computers play a big role in all aspects of music creation, from composing to production. What previously took a recording studio full of heavy equipment can now be accomplished on a laptop computer. Musicians today must be knowledgeable about the possibilities and limitations of the most current technology, which evolves constantly.

The turning point for the digital musical revolution came around 1980. That was when MIDI (Musical Instrument Digital Interface) was widely adopted, the compact disc replaced vinyl, and analogue tape started to be replaced with digital recording. Today, most music is produced using *sequencers* and *synthesizers*, with recording, notation, and mixing software programs such as Logic, Pro Tools, Sibelius, and Finale.

As mentioned, some artists prefer the warm sound offered by analogue tape recording and will still lay tracks on tape recorders, "dumping" them into a digital program such as Pro Tools to be mixed and mastered. Interestingly, there have been minimal advances in sound production technology used in amplifiers and speakers, at least when compared to the digital revolution in music technology and production.

Musical Services: Work for Hire

Is music a product or a service? While artists tend to consider their songs and recordings as a product to be marketed, sold, and licensed, music is also used for many other purposes, as we discussed in the first chapter. We might create music to be used in a movie or video game or to be played in the background at a spa or a healing center. We hear music as advertising *jingles* daily. Music as a component of visual media is of course nothing new: Silent movies were originally accompanied by a pianist or small combo in the theater while the movie played, and film scores for iconic movies such as Star Wars (by John Williams) have become legendary. Video game music is its own category.

The composer, producer, arranger, and performer are often hired to provide a service. We call this *work for hire* as recognition that the musician is not entitled to future recurring revenues, or royalties, from the work. A general business band performing at a wedding is understood to be performing work for hire. For the session musician, the bulk of their work might be work for hire. If they are self-employed, they will sell their performance to the highest bidder, as a service for fee. It's a useful example for some musicians, as not all musicians can earn passive income from royalties.

When a musician does work for hire, it should pay a reasonable amount of money. Sometimes, as with scoring a film, the composer may not have a choice of how the working agreement is structured and compensated. The preference and budget of the film producer will indicate whether or not it makes sense to create the music as work for hire or as a product that the composer will continue to profit from. If the movie is a blockbuster, it's always better for the composer to retain ownership of the score, as their earnings will be exponentially higher. But if the movie is a flop, they might be better off taking a flat fee as work for hire. The fact is, nobody can predict whether or not a movie will be successful.

In a completely different setting, *music therapy* is an ancient practice which uses music for healing. More recently, it's become an integral practice used by clinical treatment teams in modern hospitals.

Horizontal Versus Vertical Expansion

I've found many musicians aren't aware of the distinction between horizontal and vertical expansion. These terms describe ways in which a company can expand their offerings of products or services.

A vertical expansion is when a business sells new products or services in the same category or expands into another area of their supply chain. For example, a car company could decide to build trucks, or go into the tire business. A suit designer might decide to offer accessories, hats, or shoes.

In music, concertizing could be a vertical expansion for an artist who has previously only created recordings. Or a musician could start a booking agency or a record label.

Horizontal expansion is when a business offers new products or services that are from a different category. For example, a pop star starts a fashion clothing or fragrance line. Rapper and entrepreneur Jay-Z expanded into the sports consultancy business, recently signing up the NFL as a client. The concept of horizontal and vertical expansion can be a useful one for music businesses and for musicians.

CRM Software

CRM, also known as *Customer* (or *Client*) *Relationship Management*, is a critical aspect of marketing and sales in the business world. Imagine you have several prospects for hiring your band for events. Likely you will have no problem remembering who you spoke with last, when you spoke with them, and what you discussed. Now, multiply the number of prospects by a factor of 10 or 100. You will need a system to keep track of when you last spoke, and where you left things in the process. We discussed this previously in the chapter on networking, with the tickler file.

For bands, artists, writers, agents, managers, and other intermediaries, a regular newsletter delivered by e-mail is a way of staying in touch with fans, collaborators, and partners. Social media messaging should be integral to your promotional strategy. This is where CRM software comes in handy. There are many choices for this, such as Bandzoogle, Hubspot, Survey Monkey, Hootsuite, Constant Contact, and Salesforce. CRM software is usually offered on a *freemium* basis, meaning there is a free version, but to scale up or get access to all features you must pay a monthly subscription. Some programs work better for smaller or larger business models. You will need to do some research to find out which is the best solution for you.

Blockchain Technology

There's been a lot of hype about *blockchain technology* and *cryptocurrencies* in the last years. While we are still a ways off from realizing the potential of these new mediums of exchange, blockchain does hold out the promise of consolidating the transfer of digital music and the payments for it into a single channel. It's possible, and maybe even likely that this technology will solve the problem of not having a central clearinghouse for global music rights and payments. We shall see. Cryptocurrencies as a means of payment, while gaining in popularity, is still relatively controversial due to questions of security and lack of government controls.

This list of trends is not complete; it's meant to show a representative smattering of recent possibilities and challenges that will change over time. Ideally, you'll consider what other new developments could be just around the corner. We can't know what the future holds, but we know it will be different.

CHAPTER 13

A&R, Streaming for Artists, How to Publish Your Music and Get It on Spotify

The path to stardom for bands used to depend on producing a "label showcase" to prove to the record companies, agents, and promoters that a wildly enthusiastic audience already appreciated the group's music and that they could put on an energetic performance to support the sales of their recorded music. It was seen as a rite of passage to rent the club, produce the show, get the fans packed in, and impress the all-powerful A&R representative. This is how bands got signed. The internet has changed all that.

What Is A&R and How Do Bands Get Signed?

A&R stands for *Artist and Repertoire* and was originally a role within record companies for identifying, attracting, and developing musical talent for the record labels. A&R roles have evolved as the music industry has changed. While A&R jobs do still exist, the modern A&R representative does not necessarily work exclusively for the record company. They might also manage bands, promote clubs, or run small record labels.

Since the adoption of the internet, file sharing, and streaming services by musicians, the types of deals have changed, favoring distribution and 360-deals (where the labels claim a portion of everything the artist earns). Though record company backing can be a badge of credibility, especially with booking agents, not all bands or artists choose to sign with a label.

Today, with the ability of musicians to connect directly with their fans on the internet, the A&R's role diminished from its heyday. Conversely, the A&R role comprises a broader scope of activities. While the old school model of A&R reps matching artists with songs and labels has largely disappeared, A&R reps still play relevant roles in the music industry. A&R has changed, but it's not going away anytime soon.

With a dearth of label signings, A&R reps often work independently, partnering with artists, bands, and smaller labels to identify and sign talent, develop and refine their music, and help them market directly to their fans. The line has become blurred between A&R, live concert and studio production, artist management, artist development, publishing, distribution, and music marketing. The A&R of today wears many hats, though the traditional A&R model still survives. The major labels have retained their A&R departments, though in a diminished role, and rely on the services of talented A&R reps. Since fewer acts are signed to big label deals these days, fewer of these reps work inside record companies.

Who Does A&R?

Some A&R reps step into the role as musicians. While not absolutely required, it's desirable for reps to have backgrounds as either artists or songwriters and have specialized knowledge and experience with artist development, music promotion, and the creative musical process. You're probably working in some facet of A&R if you find yourself actively developing talent, helping musicians connect to their fan base, getting them signed to a label, getting their music published, finding them music placements, or promoting them.

In a label, A&Rs function at different levels, depending on the size of the company. Entry-level reps may be responsible for scouting talent, and then making recommendations to management. Higher-level managers in A&R are tasked with making the initial contact with the artist or band, and may also be authorized to sign them to the label. Signing of artists usually must be approved by higher-ups in the company. If you're an unsigned band looking for a label, or a musician wanting to work in A&R, you should learn about the various roles played by A&R reps, and get to know some of them personally, if possible.

The Roles of A&R: Finding Talent and More

The traditional A&R is a gatekeeper and scout. As the point of contact with the label in contract negotiations, their job is to find marketable music for the company to produce and sell. Scouting new talent requires going to clubs and concerts, networking with studios and producers, and getting to know various music scenes, whether local, college-oriented, style-based, or online. The *talent scout* reads industry publications and listens to demo submissions. The A&R works directly with artists and bands to get them ready to springboard their career. Since scouting talent is usually fun, and you get to meet interesting people, the A&R job seems glamorous.

Besides record companies, publishers also employ A&R reps to find and sign talent to publishing deals. There can be more money in publishing and licensing than in performing, or streaming sales, so labels will often try to stake a claim to an artist's publishing and master rights. (We will discuss publishing in more depth later in this chapter.) A *360-deal* is when labels claim a portion of an artist's publishing, performing, and merchandising revenues, in addition to the *mechanicals* (royalties) from the master recordings used in visual media. Publishing A&Rs work to sign songwriters and then get their songs placed for licensing or recording. The A&R will be the liaison between the business affairs department of the record company or publisher and the artist's attorney.

Pro Tip:
Always hire a qualified entertainment attorney to represent you in any recording or publishing contract negotiation, and never sign anything you don't understand completely.

Overseeing the Recording Process and Artist Development

While the A&R is responsible for finding and signing new talent, the job doesn't end there. A&R reps work closely with the artist during the recording process. They help with selecting songs, choosing a producer, and finding a studio for recording. They act as the record company's representative during the recording process, and they may be involved in decisions affecting the production process.

Any decision or action which needs to occur prior to the record being released might be included in the job of the A&R. Examples include:

- Handling of payments to the artist or recording studio
- Booking the recording sessions
- Approving personnel and artistic decisions
- Arranging catering

In making decisions and assisting the recording process, the A&R acts as an intermediary between the band and the label, representing the interests of the label.

Many of these A&R roles are classified as *artist development*. Artist development is a much broader term than A&R, and includes business planning, artistic direction, performance training, marketing decisions, finance, and other areas as outlined in this book. Some A&Rs work as *artist development consultants*, assisting artists with all aspects of their music career.

Assisting With Marketing and Promotion

As record companies take on less of a role with new artist development, and artists have assumed more responsibility, modern A&Rs take a part in crafting the image identity of the artist to appeal to the target audience. The musical style must be communicated clearly so it will resonate with the fans. Every artist needs a back story and a branding strategy to attract and maintain fan engagement. A good example of this might be how Motown trained their performers and transformed them into cohesive acts. Artists need support from the label to create and manage their promotional strategies, and this becomes the job of the A&R.

Independent A&R

As mentioned, A&R roles have changed drastically with the transformation of the music industry in the digital age. Due to the internet, direct-to-fan marketing has diminished the power of traditional A&Rs. Regardless, independent and major labels still use A&R staff to sift through the jumble of content on the internet and discover new talent.

Music supervisors and music publishers also do A&R, as most music licensed for use in film and television comes from unsigned artists. Artists should consider publishing and licensing agreements as a way to develop their careers as recording artists and live performers. For example, before pop supergroup Coldplay was signed to Capitol Records they were part of BMG Music Publishing who helped them record and shop their music to the labels.

The Future of A&R

Unsigned artists and bands are still expected to develop their fan base at the outset, typically by using social media creatively, and by playing exciting live shows. Defining A&R roles more broadly for the future industry makes sense. For example, websites and blogs can help to establish a music career, and A&R can oversee the content creation aspects. Using video, online blogs (or vlogs) with high traffic can popularize a new artist virtually overnight. High numbers of views and followers on YouTube, Instagram, TikTok, or other platforms can lend credibility and attract listeners. The band Arctic Monkeys first achieved public acclaim on MySpace, and Lorde was discovered via her SoundCloud page.

Action Steps:
1. Decide what social media channels to use.
2. If you already use social media, review your channels to see if you are regularly growing your fan base.

Events, festivals, showcases, and contests offer another way to establish fame in the music industry and provide opportunities for an unsigned band to be seen and heard by industry influencers. Some examples:

- SXSW has become a coveted venue where bands can make a splash.
- The National Association for College Activities (NACA) holds selective showcases where bands can get booked for college tours. Getting in front of college audiences has always been seen as one key to wider success for new artists.

- Songwriting contests such as the Billboard Song Contest and the John Lennon Songwriting Contest (JLSC) are also good ways to connect with record and publishing companies.
- Websites for music placement and licensing to visual media, such as Marmoset Music or Komposed, offer excellent platforms for musicians to get label attention.

These organizations all fulfill crucial A&R functions. Crowdfunding can help, too. If you can get 10,000 would-be fans to plunk down $5 to fund your next EP, that is pretty strong proof of your music's viability with a (paying) audience. While these forms of A&R might integrate with other areas in the business, such as publicity, booking, and even finance, we can consider them as being under the A&R umbrella.

What Musicians Need to Know About A&R

With disruptive changes in our industry, the roles of A&R have been transformed. As the change continues, the role of A&R will also change. Some old methods remain, such as the A&R functioning as gatekeepers at the major labels. Musicians should focus on artist development, and determine where they need help. Independent A&Rs are always looking for artists and bands to promote, sell, produce, and otherwise shape into successful acts. You need a team that believes in your music as much as you do, and will be focused on achieving the next steps for your climb to fame. You could find that person anywhere, but they are likely already working in the music industry, perhaps as an A&R rep.

The tenure of an A&R at record companies tends to be short, especially if the acts they sign don't turn into major successes. Most label A&R reps don't last long. When they do jump ship (or are fired), they might make an excellent manager due to their specialized knowledge and list of contacts.

Action Step:
As you learn all you can about the business, take the time to learn about A&R, how it works, who does it, and where to connect with A&R reps, as you build out your network.

How to Get Your Music Published

Professional musicians, composers, songwriters, arrangers, and producers all face the same issues and challenges in getting their music out to the general public and getting paid for the use of their music through licensing and publishing deals. While the issues surrounding monetizing intellectual property are indeed myriad and complex, the solutions don't have to be. Newcomers to the business should carefully research solutions, and learn everything they can about how to get paid through publishing and licensing music.

As you learn, you should consult with professional musicians with direct experience, and you will need a good music lawyer and an accountant. The solution is usually to either start your own publishing company, or depend on someone else's company. You could also do both these things. The costs are not high to start your own company, but there are some steps to get to the point when you are ready.

What Is Intellectual Property and How Is It Protected?

The U.S. Constitution states that protection of ownership for works of intellectual property should be provided for in the laws made by Congress. The Founding Fathers included this provision because they understood there would be a need to incentivize progress in science and "useful arts" for the good of society. The original laws made by the Congress sought to protect inventions and creative works of art or authorship by providing for patents and copyrights, respectively. Nowadays, inventions are typically still covered by patents, while works of art or authorship are protected using copyrights. The most recent update to copyright laws was the Music Modernization Act of 2018 (MMA), as we also discussed earlier.

For a written or recorded work, two copyrights exist: one for the composition and one for the recording (the latter is called *master rights,* or sometimes *mechanical license* when used together with visual media). To qualify for protection, a work must be either written down or recorded by some means, usually audio or video. For example, if I recite a poem or sing a song I made up out of my head, and that's the only place it exists, it will not qualify for protection under copyright. If I write it down, the composition is automatically protected by a *simple* or *compulsory* copyright. I can also get a more formal copyright as additional proof that I wrote it. If I choose to record the composition, then an additional copyright will apply to the recorded version of the song, as mentioned earlier.

The term *music publishing* refers to the structure of ownership along with the process by which it is protected, licensed, distributed, or otherwise sold. Some exceptions exist to the protections provided by copyright, such as *fair use* (as in education) and *de minimis* (use of a small amount), but explaining these in more depth goes beyond the scope of this book.

Getting Started With Publishing Your Music

Assuming you have a song or collection of songs already composed, written down, or recorded, you should take the proper steps to protect your intellectual property. This is a prudent and wise business decision. Where to begin? You will need to do a little research on the types of business entities available and the performing rights organizations (PROs) you might consider using. The basic steps are:

1. Form your business entity (we discussed how to do this in Chapter 6)
   a. Find or invent a name.
   b. File for a d.b.a. (a.k.a. business certificate "doing business as").
   c. Consider various business structures, that is, LLC, LLP, C-Corporation.
2. Open a business bank account.
3. Register with a PRO.

This might seem simple at first look, yet the decisions can be quite complex. Let's have a closer look at each step.

What Name Should You Use?

Perhaps the most important, and most difficult aspect of starting any business, is settling on an appropriate name. Let me rephrase that: We need to find the perfect name. The name of your business is the one thing you'd like people to remember. If they don't remember your name, how will they ever find you? It's not easy to come up with a good name that will stick in the memory of your prospects. For one thing, most good names are already taken.

At this point, you may ask, couldn't I just use my own name? While this may work for the artist part of your business, it isn't the best idea to use your own name for a publishing company, for the following reasons:

- Having your name front and center could hurt the potential for copublishing deals, as writers collaborating with you on songs or productions might be turned off by this arrangement.
- Your name may not be particularly memorable.
- You might want to separate your personal life from your business life for privacy reasons.

Since a lot of good names will be taken, I have a tried and true solution for you: Make up a new word. As mentioned earlier, companies like Kleenex, Verizon, Comcast, and Xerox are examples of companies that chose this option. A friend of mine called his publishing company Daa-Doo Music and has had success publishing books and recordings using that moniker. Use of acronyms is not generally recommended, although companies such as IBM and AT&T have taken this approach. The issue with acronyms is that people forget what they stand for—do you instantly recall that IBM stands for International Business Machines?

Branding professionals can name your company for you and create all your image identity materials (logo, website landing page, business cards, social media accounts), but they can be quite expensive, charging many thousands. With some effort, research, and creativity, you should be able to come up with a good name on your own.

Action Step:
Show your top three naming ideas to friends to get their impressions.

Pro Tip:
If the domain is available as a dot-com, the name will likely be available for business use, since almost everyone in business has registered their name as a dot-com domain.

Register Your Publishing Company Name

This part should be fairly easy. You will need to file as a d.b.a. which stands for "doing business as." To do this, first download a blank *business certificate* form from the Web, or pick one up at any office supply store. This one-page form asks for your name and address and a brief description of your intended business activities (music publishing, music services, etc.), plus your proposed business name. You must sign the form in the presence of a *notary public*. The notary will check your identification and compare your signature, to legally confirm your identity. They will sign your form with you, then they will put their embossed stamp over the signature. That's it.

Pro Tip:
Never pay for a notary, because your bank or school provides this service for free.

After you fill out the form, and with the notary stamp in place, go to the office of the clerk of the county or city court to register your business. They will do a final check to make sure nobody else is using your chosen name for a similar type of business in your area, and then you pay a small one-time fee to register your business with the court. It varies by county and city, but the fee is usually between $30.00 and $60.00 to file your business registration with the clerk of the court.

Why file? You will need the business certificate to open a business banking account, as a way to separate your business and personal finances. This will make your accounting and taxes much easier. Business registration will also protect your own use of the name. You can stop others from using your name or similar names that could be confusing to the public, and you can protect your own use of the name if you are ever challenged on it. Finally, you need a business banking account to join a *performing rights organization* (PRO) so they can pay you your royalties.

Structure of Your Business

At this point you are what is known as a *sole proprietor*. This means you are the only owner of your business. I'll put that another way: You ARE your business. Registering as a d.b.a. protects your business name from infringement, and allows you to have a business banking account. You need the business banking account to receive your royalties and simplify your accounting.

Some sole proprietors take the next step and register their company with the state as a limited liability company (LLC). As we saw in chapter 6, this offers a *corporate veil* which protects personal assets from liability from lawsuits. Instead of forming an LLC, it's possible to purchase business liability insurance. This might be cheaper than forming an LLC. For most people starting out, the d.b.a. is the best solution, though there may be benefits from other forms of incorporation such as the ability to issue shares of stock in your company.

Action Step:
Decide on your preferred business structure for your publishing.

Choose Your Performing Rights Organization (PRO)

After you've chosen a name, registered as a business, and opened your business banking account, it's time to affiliate with (join) a PRO. The three main ones in the United States are:

1. ASCAP (American Society of Composers, Authors, and Publishers)
2. BMI (Broadcast Music, Inc.)
3. SESAC (Society of European Stage Authors and Composers)

To join, you pay a one-time membership fee, and submit a catalogue of your musical works to them, so they can track usage and pay you the royalties they collect on your behalf. Research the PRO before making your decision, because each uses different processes.

Action Steps:
1. Contact each PRO directly, speak with a membership associate, gather information, read some blogs and articles, and gain an understanding of how each one works.
2. Compare the specific requirements, benefits, and costs.
3. Ask others who they use, and why.

Your Publishing Is in Place, Now What?

Your publishing company works like a cash register in a shop. It collects money, so you can get paid for your music compositions, songs, arrangements, and productions—whether from syndication (licensing), performances, sales of recordings, streaming, or any other use of your music. Owning your publishing will cause others to view you as being more serious about your career. When you own your publishing, you increase your credibility as an artist-entrepreneur. It shows you are taking charge of your financial destiny. Of course, you still need to actively market and sell or license your work to earn money.

Music supervisors match visual media content with music. They work for the producers of films, television shows, and advertising, serving clients with very specific needs, budgets, and timelines. It's a challenging job, and you should package and present your music to them to help them succeed in suggesting your music to their clients. Websites such as marmosetmusic.com let you post your music, and an algorithm will match your music to videos needing music based on style and intensity. Building and leveraging your professional network will also help you get placements for your music in visual and other media.

Action Steps:
Think through all the steps, and learn as much as you can, so you understand your decisions and why you are making them. Starting your own music publishing company is a milestone on the path to success for composers, arrangers, songwriters, and producers.

Streaming for Dollars: How to Use Spotify

As a musician, you're always working to get your music out to fans. You've invested a lot of time and energy to create music you truly believe in, and you are actively connecting with your audience. In the digital age, It's easier than ever to get your music online and gain fans using streaming services. I'm often asked about how artists can get their music onto Spotify, one of the most popular streaming music platforms. It's not hard to do, but there are some technical requirements and procedures, which I will describe here.

To earn money streaming, it's not enough to merely upload your music. You'll need to promote it. Fortunately, there are plenty of online resources to help you to market your music and engage with fans. Spotify offers useful tools to enhance your chances for success. Streaming on Spotify and other platforms can build your fan base and help you earn money. It should be a part of your overall strategy for moving forward with your music career.

What Is Spotify?

Spotify is a music streaming service which uses a *freemium* model. The free version subjects listeners to ads, similar to YouTube. Like other freemium platforms, Spotify tries to get users to upgrade to a premium subscription, currently priced at $9.99 per month or $4.99 for students. Headquartered in Sweden, Spotify serves over 60 regions globally. Music can be browsed on the platform using genre, artist, and album, and playlists are generated and shared via social media. As of 2020, Spotify provides access to more than 50 million songs for 286 million active users worldwide, of which 130 million are paying subscribers, accounting for 36 percent of the global music streaming market.

Spotify pays artist royalties based on the number of streams of their songs as a proportion of total songs streamed on the platform. This is different from traditional song royalties, which calculate fixed payments to artists based on the number of times a song is played, or a recording is sold. While Spotify has received criticism from artists such as Taylor Swift and Thom Yorke, who claim artists are not compensated fairly, the company announced in 2016 that it had paid out over $5 billion to the music industry, representing 70 percent of its revenues. They promised to pay out another $2 billion over the following two years. According to recent news reports, they paid out much more than that in 2017 alone. A study showed that the bulk of Spotify's revenues are paid to independent labels, not artists, and the labels keep a significant portion of the money. While this has been good for the labels, it hasn't helped the artists as much.

While artists have complained that they are not paid fairly for their streams, in its defense, Spotify claims to be beneficial to musicians and their labels by working to lure listeners away from piracy sites, while encouraging them to upgrade to premium listening services. Overall, the music industry feels that Spotify has been beneficial because it offers a new revenue model for music. Since revenues from recorded music had fallen to historic lows, the consensus is that anything that gets people paying even small amounts for listening to music is positive.

Streaming has increased revenues from recorded music over the last several years. After many years of losing money, Spotify turned a profit in 2019 and strives to be the dominant player in streaming music subscription services.

Music Labels, Aggregators, and Digital Distribution

Good news: You don't have to be signed to a label to get paid for streaming your music on Spotify. If you are signed to a label, the company will get your music uploaded to Spotify. If you aren't on a label, you can directly upload your music to Spotify's site if you have the ability to license your music (more on that next). An aggregator, such as Tunecore or CD Baby, can easily get your music streamed on multiple sites.

Action Steps:
Spotify lists their preferred digital music distributors (called *aggregators*) on their website. Take a look at aggregators' websites and find their step-by-step instructions to get you started. Using the *Spotify for Artists* page on the Spotify website you can learn from a series of helpful videos covering the basics of how to upload and promote your music, form your team, and use Spotify to your advantage.

How to Upload Your Music

Before submitting music to Spotify, you should check the following:

1. You must own the master recording rights.
2. Songs using samples must have the permission from the owner of any sampled music.
3. For covers or songs written with someone else, you must have permission from the other writer(s).

4. You must have the rights to any artwork you use, and make sure to check the specs on any images you submit with the recording.

5. Make sure your name is spelled correctly so your music doesn't end up on multiple profiles (this happens a lot).

It takes five business days for your music to be available for streaming on the site while Spotify checks that sound quality is good and that the music will be discoverable.

While it's easy to upload your music, to make the most of it you will need well-defined strategies to promote your music and regularly engage with your listeners.

Make Your Spotify Game Plan: Artist Profile

When you upload your music, you'll need a solid game plan to help your audience find you. You want people to know who you are, and it's up to you to tell them. Your *artist profile* on Spotify is like a quiver, filled with arrows to aim at your target audience. It's designed to help you create a buzz to initiate and maintain audience engagement.

First impressions matter. Your artist profile will show audiences who you are and what you do. It's where listeners go to connect with you and your music. Use your Spotify artist profile to create a personal brand that feels natural and unique. Profiles include an artist bio (1,500 words, max), avatar image, background image, and photo gallery for promo shots or concert photos. You can list your concert and gig dates. Spotify will post these automatically if you have tickets for sale on Ticketmaster, Songkick, AXS, or Eventbrite. Live gig listings will also show up on your fans' personalized concert section. You can even sell concert merch through Spotify.

According to Troy Carter, head of Creative Services at Spotify, one key to success with streaming is having good music. A strong belief in your product will help you and others to promote it. Use your artist profile to show your passion and dedication and to tell listeners why they should care and be interested in you and your music.

More Resources to Promote Your Music: Playlists and Social Media

Besides the artist profile, Spotify offers more resources to get your hustle going, create a buzz, and directly engage listeners. Two of these are *playlists* and *artist's pick*. These are designed to keep fans coming back to listen to your music again and again. The artist playlist tells fans what you are listening to, and the artist's pick is a song or album which can be pinned to the top of your playlist.

Action Steps:
Use playlists and artist's pick to show off your music, or to share what you're listening to at the moment with your fans. Add a line of text to the artist's pick to promote a live gig.

Stay active on Spotify by making changes to your playlist, especially if you can't release new music every week or month. Tweaking your playlist helps with fan engagement. Playlists create community on social media and stimulate interaction with your fans. Fans can make listening recommendations for you and other playlist followers. Think of it as your own radio show, where you get to express yourself through ongoing curation of the music you listen to and love. A dynamic playlist helps fans feel connected with you and appreciate your work even more. Also, the more fans add your songs to their own Spotify playlists, the more likely that the site's editors and algorithms will notice and add your music to even bigger playlists.

Spotify's website shares some useful strategies for using social media platforms together with Spotify:

1. Plan around your calendar. Studio sessions, video productions, interviews, creative meetings, and travel all provide opportunities to craft a compelling story and visual for each event.
2. Time your releases carefully. Releasing music frequently is a good way to attract new listeners as Spotify urges fans to look for new music using their *Release Radar* function, plus their Friday new music playlist.

3. Use your personal network. Direct message all your contacts asking them to share your music. Monitor your sharing and viewing activity carefully.

4. Use *Calls to Action* (CTAs) to drive regular traffic to your artist page on Spotify. Tell fans where to go to listen to your music.

5. Use incentives with your CTAs. Offer your most engaged fans chances to win merch or special music.

6. Use *Follow CTAs* before releases, so fans will get notifications every time you release new music.

Action Steps:

Everyone starts out listening to your music as a passive fan. It's your job to convert them to the active fan who enthusiastically shares your music with others. Achieve this by engaging your fans with continual and interesting messaging to reinforce their connection with you.

Other Tools to Engage Your Audience: Spotify Codes and Data Analytics

Spotify Codes are scannable QR codes that link to your song, album, playlist, or artist page. Codes can be put on posters, flyers, stickers, postcards, confetti, or business cards which could be passed out at shows. These codes allow listeners to later hear a song on Spotify that they enjoyed at your show.

Spotify offers data analytics tools as resources. The *Artist Insights* page shows the data to help you time your releases for maximum effect. For example, a good time to release a new single might be when interest is peaking from a previous release. Use data tools on Spotify to track your fan engagement, to gain insights to the appeal of your music to fans, and to prolong fan engagement.

Action Step:

Become familiar with your analytics tools on Spotify.

Who's on Your Team?

In the music business, you need a team. One of the more interesting videos on the Spotify for Artists website is called *Building Your Team*. On the video, Spotify employees talk about your potential team members, such as an accountant, manager, lawyer, booking agent, and road manager. They point out that every artist's needs are different, and the composition of your team depends on where you are in your career. Although we've discussed this in previous sections of the book, a few points from the video bear repeating:

1. Once you have music you believe in, your team should be as hungry as you are.
2. When building your team, look for people who share your passion for your music, because you are asking them to care about your art and craft as much as you do.
3. You should be the hardest working member of the team, since nobody can care about your music more than you do.

Action Steps:

After submission, consider your best strategies for releasing tracks, frequency and timing of releases, sharing on social media, building your artist profile, using playlists, and effectively engaging with your audience.

CHAPTER 14

Odds and Ends: Making Recordings, the Sound Check, and Teaching Music

Making Professional Recordings

Recorded music is the ultimate product in our industry next to concert performances. Musicians work painstakingly to produce excellent recordings, whether to use as professional demos, for downloads, on CDs, for streaming, in music videos, to add to visual media, or to register and document their music.

The highly technical fields of music production and engineering draw on science and art to produce artistically successful and high-quality recordings. Musicians should learn all they can about the recording process, so they can create professional-level recordings. With a laptop and some good software, it's possible to produce them in your bedroom. For our purposes, I am addressing the specific challenges related to recording groups of musicians live and in the recording studio.

At some risk of oversimplification, we could say there are three stages to creating a recording: *preproduction*, *production*, and *postproduction*. This is how most professionals define the recording process.

Preproduction

The moment you have decided to make a recording you are already in preproduction! *Preproduction* describes everything that needs to happen, including all the decisions to be made, up until the first notes are actually recorded. In fact, preproduction can sometimes take longer than the other two stages combined and almost always takes much longer than you might expect. Many artists take as much as a year or more in the preproduction stage to make a record.

I've listed some of the kinds of decisions and activities associated with preproduction as follows. My list isn't exhaustive; it's meant only to give some idea of what needs to happen before starting to record:

- Choose material to be recorded
- Choose musicians
- Arrange music for the recording
- Schedule rehearsals
- Investigate potential recording studios or remote recording sites
- Gather reference tracks
- Secure permission from owners of rights of any music not composed by you
- Choose caterer for session, find out about musicians' dietary needs
- Talk to graphic artists and photographers about artwork and design of materials
- Choose a recording engineer
- Talk to web designer about website (as applicable)
- Choose a videographer to capture some scenes in the studio and/or make a music video
- Estimate budget items line by line; create total budget
- Procure budget
- Book studio dates
- Decide about recording methods, tracking, software, and so on
- Consider transportation needs of musicians and instrument transport
- Complete "trial" or practice recordings of basic tracks
- Learn the music (!)

Close attention to all the details of preproduction increases the likelihood that your recording goes smoothly and the results are satisfying.

Choosing a Studio

Every studio is different with so many things to consider such as the physical space, equipment, personnel, location, and sound. Consider the following as you evaluate studios:

- Are the lines of sight workable for your session?
- Is the equipment well maintained, and does it meet your needs?
- What instruments and microphones will be available for your session?
- Is the engineer included in the cost of the rental?
- If you have to load equipment into the studio, is it difficult to do so?
- Is there parking available?
- How much does the studio cost per hour or per day?

Have a checklist prepared in advance, along with a list of questions. Plan to tour multiple studios, and leave enough time to ask your questions. Forgetting to ask an important question can lead to unpleasant surprises later. Listen to recordings that were made in the studio, and if possible, witness a portion of an actual session, or at least hear some of their work in progress.

For remote recordings on location, you will need to spend some time there at the times of day you plan to record, to see what is going on in the area and check for ambient noise. Consider the logistics of moving equipment in and out, including the required set up and teardown time. Wherever you choose to record, you'll likely find there is no perfect place to make recordings. Make all your decisions based on a careful comparison of the positives and negatives.

Action Step:
Write a preproduction plan for a recording you plan to make. Include as many details as you can think of.

Production

Getting in the studio and recording the tracks is the fun part. The process is rewarding, exciting, and at times, frustrating. Not everything turns out the way you expect. Your attention to preproduction means you've prepared yourself and your team for most foreseeable issues. The things you didn't anticipate will rise up to present new challenges. Be prepared for contingencies, be flexible, and expect the unexpected. Hope for the best and prepare for the worst.

I recommend you record more songs than you actually plan to use. This way you can keep only the best work. If you intend to have 12 songs for release, it is a good idea to record about 20. This way, when a track doesn't turn out the way you expect, you can put it aside. Only use the best tracks. If you recorded 20 tracks, you can pick the best 12 to 15 for overdubs and mixing. If you need six tracks for an EP, plan to record at least 10 to 12 to start.

Have a Plan to Follow

In preparing for battle, Dwight D. Eisenhower said that "…plans are useless, but planning is indispensable." Always develop a cohesive recording plan in the preproduction phase, mapping out each step carefully. Start by recording basic rhythm section tracks live with a "scratch" vocal used as a guide; the final vocal can be rerecorded later. Plan on retreating to the control booth often to listen in between takes, to hear how it's turning out, and what adjustments in the playing you could make to improve the recording. If a track sounds good overall, but there are a few mistakes, you can always punch in and out for a single instrument to fix a few notes or bars. Sometimes if it's just one wrong note, you can change it with a software program, like Pro Tools.

After recording the basic tracks and fixing mistakes, usual next steps are to overdub vocals, solos, and doublings. Layering new parts and adding *sweetening* such as strings, synths, percussion, and hand-claps can also be done. Attention should be paid to *effects* (signal processing) and *panning* (left and right, or surround sound), with an ear toward what the final mix might sound like. The person responsible for the many decisions during this stage is usually the *producer*. An *executive producer* might be the person who funds the recording while a producer working under an artist-producer might be called a *line producer*. Some artists are self-produced.

Postproduction

Mixing is the final part of the production phase and is the transition to postproduction. *Postproduction* begins when all (or most) of the tracks have been recorded and mixed. Decisions made during mixing affect the sound of the final recording. The mixing engineer chooses the volume, effects, panning, timbre, and placement for every note on the recording. Everyone hears music differently, so it's a challenge to create a mix that everyone will be happy with. The *final mix* should not obscure or downplay the most crucial elements of the recording. It should bring out the best of the recorded tracks in a cohesive, pleasing whole.

Mastering

After crafting the final mix comes the *mastering*. This highly specialized function should be done by an engineer with experience in this area. In mastering, there are more crucial decisions to be made. How much silence should there be between each of the tracks on the record? What should the overall volume and dynamic range be like? Are all songs at the same volume or are some louder than others?

The mastering engineer ensures the dynamic range is appropriate throughout the recording, that the songs aren't too loud at their loudest or too soft at their softest, and that all the songs fit onto the disc with a small section of silence between them (i.e., if making a physical copy of the recording). All the tracks on the record need to be balanced in overall volume. It isn't as easy as it sounds. A fresh set of ears is essential for mastering, so while it's fine for the recording engineer to create the final mix, you need a separate specialist to do mastering. Most mastering engineers charge on a per-song basis.

Action Step:
Research mastering engineers and how much they charge.

Other Postproduction Considerations

Besides mixing and mastering, the postproduction stage includes *duplication* (for physical copies), artwork and jacket design, photographs, and also promotional plans surrounding the release of the recordings, whether for a label or for an independent release. Duplication can be expensive for small numbers, but due to economy of scale, ordering more copies lowers the cost of each one. Artwork has to be proofed, and decisions must be made about format, printing, fonts, and colors. Liner notes need to be written, pictures finally selected, and you'll likely feel some pressure to get it done quickly, as you've been working on your project for so long and can't wait to get it finished. This is not the time to rush to decisions, because you will have to live with this product the rest of your life, and you don't want to have regrets.

Don't forget the addition of meta-data to each track, and to the album, so the music can be registered for publishing houses, performing rights organizations, streaming platforms, music aggregators, and point of sale. Consider your best options for distribution, as we've discussed elsewhere in this book.

Listen and Enjoy

Finally, you have your recording. You should be able to listen to your recording and enjoy it. If you love it, that is enough reward. If you don't like it, why would anyone else? It is useful to think about your art this way: You make it for you. Chances are, if you like it, so will others.

Most likely, when you listen to your recordings you'll notice some things you aren't completely happy with. Ask yourself what you would do differently next time, and make a note of it. You will have more opportunities to work in the studio, and you shouldn't make the same mistakes again. Mistakes are an opportunity to learn what not to do.

Every recording is a learning opportunity. You can improve in the future because of all you learned, and you will fix anything that you found lacking in your previous work. With more experience, you find what works best for you, and learn to improve your process and your results. I've heard artist-producers say their feelings about their recordings are like feelings one has for their children. They are releasing them into the world for everyone to see and hear and are fully aware of their qualities, strengths, and imperfections.

Let's now turn our attention to the concert stage.

Concertizing: How to Conduct a
Professional Sound Check

You arrive at the hall, all your gear is onstage, and your band is there, too. From the moment of arrival, to the opening notes of the concert, there's a lot of work to do. To produce a smooth show, with all singers and musicians comfortable on stage, and the audience enraptured with your music, you will need a thorough *sound check*. Like every other part of your performance, this requires planning.

I'll use the following scenario to explain how to do a professional sound check in a medium- or large-sized venue, theater, or hall. I'll assume there's a full *rhythm section*—guitars, keys, bass, and drums, with added hand percussion, horns, and possibly strings. We'll include a vocalist or multiple vocalists, and background vocals. This won't cover every possibility, but my basic method is adaptable to most situations and combinations of instruments.

My goal is to give the audience as natural a musical experience as possible, and to make sure the musicians on stage can hear each other and themselves. As a concert producer and music director for thousands of live gigs, I've distilled the preparation, setup, and sound check into distinct, proven steps.

Three parts of the sound check are:

1. Your plan;
2. Your procedures for front of house (FOH);
3. Your stage monitor adjustments.

These follow a logical sequence. You should memorize the process, and do it exactly the same way each time. The time required varies by group size and complexity of the music, the room acoustics, and the competency of your stage crew and sound engineer, and should take a few hours to do properly. Sometimes, we use an entire day and evening prior to the show to do a thorough sound check. Other times we must work very quickly, and get it all done in an hour or less. Every venue and show is unique, and your challenge as the leader is to make the most of each situation. Always go in with a plan.

Getting Started: Make a Plan

You want to be as prepared as possible, because you should expect to hit some snags as you go. Having no plan is a recipe for disaster. When we're producing a concert, the clock is ticking and we can't afford to waste valuable time. Inevitably, problems occur during the sound check, so you'll need extra time for troubleshooting. The better you can anticipate difficulties and leave time to troubleshoot, the less stressed you will feel as the clock ticks down to the opening curtain.

Sample plan for before the day of the show:

1. Draw a detailed stage plot. (See Figure 14.1) Show approximate placement of all performers, microphones, instruments, and amplifiers. Show placement of stage monitors and which monitors will receive individual monitor mixes. Make sure the stage manager receives this in advance.

2. Confirm with technical personnel all equipment that will be available for sound and lights, including backline (amplifiers and drums), risers, monitors, microphones, and music stands. Confirm who will be responsible for setup and operation of each. Check all logistics for transport and loading of equipment not already on-site.

3. Plan staggered arrival times of musicians and setup of equipment. Usually the drummer and percussionist should arrive first and set

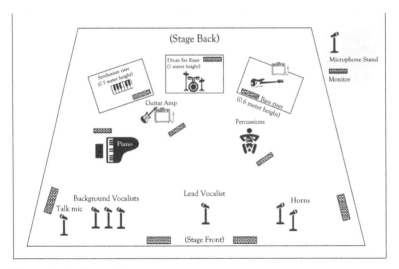

Figure 14.1 Stage plot

up their equipment. If there are any large cumbersome instruments, such as multikeyboard rigs, giant amp stacks, or a harp, they should also arrive early. Next to arrive are guitarists, then horn players, strings, vocalists, or any other musicians with relatively easy placement and setup requirements.

Special note: There should be a *green room* area ready by first arrival time for musicians to put their personal belongings, cases, and stage clothes. It should be confirmed in advance that this room will be accessible, heated (or cooled), and clean. Light refreshments, snacks, and beverages should be available. We want performers and crew to be comfortable during any down time. It may also be necessary to plan for a catered meal, as we don't want team members having to leave the premises to eat.

4. Select several songs in advance for the sound check. Depending on time available, there should be at least three or four selections. They should be picked specifically to hear different sections of the band, such as rhythm section, horns, and full band with vocals. Then we will need a song that includes everyone at the same time.

Special note: Another consideration for sound check song selection might be songs that need rehearsal or have technically difficult sections, such as beginnings, endings, and transitions. Do not expect to play songs in their entirety, however.

Pro Tip:
Have a production assistant on hand to call the performers to the stage in the order needed.

Action Step:
Draw a stage plot for your band set up and sound check. Include a list of all equipment needed for your concert.

Procedures for Front of House (Mains)

The term *front of house* (where the audience will be) is abbreviated as FOH. The FOH sound engineer will use a *soundboard* (or mixer) to mix all the instruments and vocals to sound good in that space. The (usually large) speakers aimed at the audience are called *mains*, meaning the main speakers. What the audience hears depends on the quality and suitability of the mains speakers and the mixing skill of the FOH engineer.

The audience should experience the music in the most natural way possible, and this is the job of the FOH engineer. The engineer must first listen carefully to each instrument separately and then faithfully recreate the sound through the mains. FOH engineers must consider the type and placement of any microphones and know how to balance signals from amplifiers and acoustic sources. They use signal processing such as *equalization* (EQ), *reverb*, *effects* (FX), and *compression* to adjust the sound, and they also make adjustments for any acoustical anomalies in the hall.

Due to the variable acoustics of the hall, the sound will be different in different parts of the audience. The engineer's job is to make the music sound good at every location in the hall. As the producer, I walk around the hall during the sound check to make sure the sound is good everywhere. If I notice deficiencies, I alert the sound engineer, so we can correct it if possible.

Running the Sound Check

The procedure for running the sound check could vary, depending on instrumentation, size of the hall, time available, and individual preferences. Over time, you will learn what works best. Following is a general description of how it might work.

Start by putting each instrument separately in turn into the mains speakers only. (Only use the stage monitors when necessary, such as with keyboards that don't have an amplifier on stage.) Have the musician play, and individually adjust the sound in the mains. Then start to combine instruments, by having them play together. Make sure each instrument plays at the same levels they will use during performance. Adjust the *levels* (volume) of each instrument first, and then adjust the EQ. The goal is to make each instrument sound as natural as possible in the speakers.

At this point, a little of each instrument could go into the stage monitor mix to make it easier for the musicians to hear each other and to check that all monitors are connected and working. If you have an experienced engineer, ask them to tell you what they need to hear as you progress through the sound check. Here's a sample order of instruments for checking the mains for FOH.

Drums (Drum Set):

Check each drum/drum microphone separately: bass drum (kick), snare, rack tom(s), floor tom(s). Then check cymbals: Place a mic on the high-hat and an overhead *condenser mic* for the rest of the cymbals. Pay close attention to the sound of each microphone and drum. If there is ringing in a drum head it may need to be dampened with some tape or baffling, the microphone placed differently, or both. The drums should be tuned at this time if they need it. There should be no effects (FX); start with a flat EQ and adjust as needed to make each drum sound the best it can. If FX are desired, they can be added at the end.

After each drum is tuned, its mic is placed, and the EQ is adjusted, have your drummer play the kick and snare together in a pattern. Balance the volume and EQ between them. Next, play fills around the toms. Then play a kick-snare groove with fills on the toms, then check the cymbals using close or overhead mics. Make certain the drummer plays at a volume level similar to during the show (this applies to all the instruments). Have the drummer play grooves and fills all around the kit for a while to achieve a balance of all the drums and cymbals that sounds good in the hall.

Note: A proper drum sound check usually takes a minimum of ½ hour; under difficult circumstances an hour or more may be needed for the drums.

Bass:

Most electric bassists use an amplifier-speaker combination on stage. It's best to use a *direct box* (DI) as opposed to the direct out from the amplifier, since the sound going to the mixing board will be more natural this way. Most direct boxes give you the option to do a *ground lift* if there is any *polarity hum*. Some higher quality amplifiers' direct out will have a ground lift (polarity switching) and give you a choice of *pre* or *post* output for the signal going to the mixing board. I always prefer the pre signal, because I'm looking for the most natural sound of the instrument to use in the mix.

If your mixing board has enough channels, you could also place a microphone on the bass amp's speaker. You can use special techniques for the placement of microphones on speakers. If you have the sound from the speaker, plus the sound directly from the instrument, you could make a blend. In most cases, the direct input from the bass through the direct box is enough. Putting another channel on the bass speaker gives you some other options for mixing. You might decide not to use the bass amp sound, as it will inevitably have some signal distortion and bleed of sound from other instruments on stage.

For an *acoustic bass*, different techniques can be used for placing the microphone, usually somewhere near the sound hole facing slightly upwards. If the bass has an internal or attached pickup, the same advice applies as for the electric. You might end up with three channels: one for the instrument's sound hole, one for the pickup, and one for the speaker.

Action Steps:

Experiment with and then use the signal paths that sound the best to create your bass mix. When checking the bass, first set the amp to a reasonable stage volume, as would be used during performance. Then have the bass player play, using the whole range of the instrument. They could play down in the low register first, then the midrange, and then up high if they are also a soloist. Adjust the timbre of the amp and set the EQ for the hall. Have the bassist play all techniques that they will use for the show, for example, slapping, finger-style, strumming, or using a pick.

Next, have the drummer and the bassist play a groove together. Adjust levels and EQ so that the balance is good in the hall and on stage.

Keyboards (Synths), Piano:

As with the bass, keyboards should go directly to the board using the keyboard's *balanced line out*, whether or not they are using an amplifier on stage for personal monitor. You don't need to place a microphone at the speaker of a keyboard amplifier. (An exception to this might be made for the Leslie speaker of a Hammond organ.) Have the keyboardist play all of the sounds and keyboards they will use. Check for levels, EQ, and distortion. Have them play in all sound levels they will be using during the concert.

For acoustic piano it is best to use two *condenser microphones* placed inside the frame, hovering over the bass and treble registers. It takes some expertise and tweaking of EQ, plus an ideal microphone placement to get a natural sound from the piano in the mix. It is usually necessary to spend some time experimenting to get the best possible sound from a piano. There are some newer ribbon-type microphones designed specifically for acoustic piano.

Note: The piano should be professionally tuned on the same day as the show.

Now have the drums and bass play with the keyboardist(s). Use one of the preselected songs from the concert.

Guitar(s):

Electric guitars should not use direct boxes. They should play through their amplifier on stage, and the speaker should have a microphone placed on it. As in the studio, sometimes both the front and back of an *open-backed speaker* may have a microphone placed on it, although in most cases for live settings this isn't really necessary. One *dynamic microphone* properly placed diagonally at the edge of the speaker cone should suffice. My favorite for this is the *Shure SM-57*, though any dynamic microphone will work.

The guitarist should play all of the sounds, levels, and effects they will be using, for example, *clean* sound, *distortion, wah-wah, chorus/flanger,* and *delays*. Each sound should be considered when making the setting at the board, and the player should strive for a balance in output (level) between sounds to make the sound engineer's job easier. For example, the distortion sound shouldn't be 10 times as loud as the clean sound. Some guitar effects using *digital modeling* might have a direct out you could experiment with using.

Acoustic guitars either have a mic placed at the sound hole or, if they have a pickup, go to a direct box and then into the mixing board. If there is an *active* (battery-powered) pickup with EQ on the guitar itself, make sure it has a fresh battery, set the volume at maximum, and the EQ flat (no boost or cuts). Once the engineer has a good sound, you can exper-iment with enhancements via the guitar pickup controls. It takes some artistry to get the best amplified sound out of acoustic instruments.

Pro Tip:
Be wary of loose jacks and old patch cables, which can create nasty unwanted pops and crackling sounds during a performance. If you need to plug or unplug the guitar cable, make sure the engineer has the channel muted first.

Horns, Strings, Auxiliary Percussion:

Horns (saxophones, trombones, trumpets, flugelhorns, flute, etc.) should be checked individually and then as a *section* if they play together as a group. Either *clip-on microphones* or mics on a stand should be pointed at the bell. Each horn should be checked playing solo, then with the horns as a group, and finally together with the rhythm section and the horn grouping. Use a piece of music preselected to showcase the horn section. Strings (violins, violas, cellos, basses) are checked in the same way. Usu-ally overheads are used, or if there is a pickup then the same procedure is followed as for acoustic guitar (using a direct box).

Percussion follows a similar procedure to the drums, with testing each instrument to be used or at least every microphone should be checked for level and EQ. This is usually much quicker than for drums because there are fewer mics. You could also check the percussion earlier in the process together with the drums.

At this point the whole band should play a song together while the engineer creates a mix. There is usually a fair amount of stopping and starting while adjustments are made. Effects, such as reverb, delays, and choruses, can be added at the mixing board at this time.

Vocals, Background Vocals

Check each vocal mic separately. Set EQ and effects. Adjust vocal mon-itors on the stage at this time. Make sure that the singers actually sing when they are checking the microphones. Just saying "testing, testing," as many singers are prone to do, is not enough for the engineer to properly adjust the microphone channel. They should sing into the mic exactly as they will be doing during the performance, without instrumental accompaniment.

Background vocals can be mixed either before or after the lead vocals. If there are multiple vocalists, each one should be assigned a separate mic, and the mic should have the EQ set specifically for their voice. They should plan on using only that mic. (This is also true for when there are multiple lead vocalists.) Next, have them sing as a group, and set levels for each to make the best possible blend for the group. Every group has a unique sound, and we always listen for that, finding the best way to enhance them in the mix.

Pro Tip:
Effects are like makeup, they are meant to enhance what is there without being too obvious.

Stage Monitors Mix

The monitor system is a separate sound system set up on the stage just for the performers. Since they are not in the hall, they can't hear what is coming out of the mains. Unlike the mains, the *monitor system* can accommodate multiple mixes, so each performer can hear only what they need. Taking the time to get a good *monitor mix* will enhance the performing experience and lead to a better, stress-free performance.

Start by adjusting each performer's mix separately as the band plays. Start with the lead vocalist, then go around to each instrument to ask what they want to hear more or less of. Set levels of each instrument in each of the separate mixes according to the preferences of each musician. EQ each monitor mix as needed. I prefer to mix monitors *dry*, meaning no reverb or effects added to the signal. Some vocalists like to hear a little reverb on their voice, and may ask for that. In most cases the natural reverb from the hall should be enough, so adding effects in the monitors isn't needed.

Pro Tip:
With stage monitors, LESS IS MORE! The less each musician can get by with from the monitor, the easier it will be for the mix engineers to do their job. The bass and drums don't need to hear everything that goes to

the FOH (front of house), for example. They just need to hear each other and enough vocal or lead instrument for reference, so they don't get lost in the arrangement. A singer may not hear their voice on stage exactly how they like but should trust they can be heard properly through the mains.

The more sound on stage coming from speakers the more *standing waves* can occur (also called *phase cancellation*, where reflecting sound waves cancel each other out). As the sound gets denser and louder, sound clarity suffers, also due to *microphone bleed* (where mics pick up other instruments than their intended one), and the harder it gets for the FOH engineer to create a good mix. Even with *in-ear monitors*, we don't always have the luxury of hearing a perfect mix on stage, the way we can in the recording studio. Professional performers do not let inadequacies in sound get in the way of delivering their best performance.

Troubleshooting and Fine-Tuning

I mentioned at the outset we should expect some problems during the sound check and be ready to solve them. Once we have the basic mix for both mains and monitors, we can do some fine-tuning. Difficulties often occur with sound in the hall and on stage, and a good engineer works quickly with the sound crew to make adjustments.

The audience and performers should be comfortable during the performance. Besides making the music sound beautiful, we want everyone, on and off the stage, to have fun. Sound issues can detract from the performers' and audience's experience during the show.

For the fine-tuning, play a few different sections of songs featuring different soloists, tempos, dynamic levels and instrument combinations. If there is more than one group performing on your equipment, be sure to memorize all backline amplifier settings so that you can adjust them back to where they were for your set. Some adjustments will need to be made in FOH when the hall is full of people, due to the *dampening* effect of the audience, but major adjustments should not need to be made on stage.

Be careful not to exhaust your performers during a long sound check. They might be tired already from travelling, and you want them to be rested up before the performance starts. Having done an effective and efficient sound check, you should now be ready to relax and have a great show!

Action Step:
Consider what has gone wrong with the sound in your previous experiences as a stage performer, and what could be done during the sound check to avoid similar problems in the future.

Entrepreneurial Music Education, Education as a Business, Building Your Career as a Music Teacher

None of us are truly unique, but our paths most certainly are. I like this expression because it causes me to reflect on my own career path, and how my experience as a music teacher might be helpful to younger musicians. I never really expected to have a career in teaching; that was just how it worked out. Many of my students aspire to teaching careers or feel teaching is in their future even if they are primarily interested in performing. I remember thinking the same way as a college music student, since I especially admired many of my own teachers. As the majority of professional musicians are called on to teach at some point in their career, I'd like to offer ideas about what it means to teach.

Teaching music can be a rewarding career. As a job, being a music educator has its share of challenges and rewards. If you decide you want to teach music, you can create your own career destination, as there are many opportunities to teach. Whether you are thinking about teaching music full time, or have thought about teaching music as a part-time *day job* while pursuing an artist career, this part of the book is for you.

Teaching Is a Vocation

Teaching music affords more than just earning potential (don't let anyone tell you there is no money in teaching). Teaching stimulates lifelong learning, helps keep you young, and gives you opportunities to interact with young people and positively impact their lives. A great teacher shows students what the future could look like for them and how their learning can help them prepare for a productive and good life.

Music is both a *vocation* (a profession, a calling) and an *avocation* (a hobby or pastime). Not every student you teach will become a professional, but music can still enrich their life in other ways. Teaching is a vocation; one is called to teach. A teacher needs specific skills and must usually undergo some training in order to be effective. Teachers need patience, creativity, strong music skills, and most importantly, they must truly care deeply about the students they teach.

Music Pedagogy

I define *pedagogy* in the simplest terms as "how to teach good" or teaching methodologies. Students come to us with different *learning styles* and capabilities. As music teachers, we should be prepared to teach all kinds of students. Learning must also be progressive; that is, there's a logical order in which foundational things should be taught and learned. Students need to crawl before they can walk, and walk before they can run. The teacher must put herself into the mindset of the student and help the student to make real and lasting progress with learning. One way we can do this is by remembering what it was like for us to learn new material, and then relearning this material together with our students.

Especially in music, students must learn to *do* things (e.g., play their instrument, read and write music, perform in a group, compose songs), so giving an explanation of how to do a specific thing is not enough. For learning to take place, the teacher must design and structure learning activities, proscribe practice routines, and then students must diligently follow those routines while correcting errors and marking their progress as they go. This process in itself is a great example of music pedagogy.

A teacher does not need to be an expert in pedagogy to succeed. Some teachers have a natural ability to improvise in the classroom, and others design very detailed and thorough lesson plans. A teacher cultivates awareness of what works best for their students and can quickly change the activity when something isn't working. Having a large arsenal of teaching techniques is a good way to prepare for being a music educator.

Just as with music, teaching requires some practice, and a good musician can usually learn to be an effective teacher. Aside from classroom management and building a curriculum, teachers will benefit from developing organized plans for their lessons. Learning about music pedagogy and writing lesson plans can stimulate teaching and learning, especially for the musician who is new to teaching.

The Business of Teaching

As you develop more teaching and musical skills, you will also need to market yourself to potential students and employers. This calls for a totally different skillset, for which creative entrepreneurial thinking can be helpful. First, understand that education is a business. Students pay tuition in order to learn, and your teaching, and their learning, is the product of your effort, skill, and knowledge. This is what you are paid for.

Fortunately, you'll find there's a strong demand for learning music, which creates the market for your teaching skills. The best teachers are always in high demand, because students know that with a good teacher, their desire for increased knowledge and training will be fulfilled. If you prepare yourself to be an educator, you will find plenty of opportunities to teach. You can always start by finding one person who wants to learn and who is willing to pay you to teach them. You don't need to think big at the outset.

As in any market, there is competition. The students and school administrators who will hire you must be able to quickly grasp why you are the best choice. At the minimum you will need a teaching resume, an artist bio, and a cover letter. If you are planning to teach private lessons independently, then you will need some marketing materials, such as a website and social media presence, plus posters, flyers, and a business card. Many teachers also produce instructional videos to promote themselves and earn money with lessons and courses online. Online teaching and learning (*distance learning*) is becoming more and more popular. This trend was accelerated by the COVID-19 pandemic.

Learn as much as you can about the education industry. If you are in college, that's a terrific place to start, using your own institution as a model. I'm not suggesting you go to business school, but it's smart to learn all you can about business, as I have stressed throughout this book. Having a mentor and learning from books and online resources can help. A mentor should lead you and help prepare you for what is ahead, plus encourage you and connect you to their own network.

Continued Lifelong Learning

My goal for each and every one of my students is for them to learn some useful things from me. I also want to learn something from each of them, so I can keep learning. As teachers, we need to stay current with the music field, because the industry changes very quickly. In preparing our students for the future, we can't rely on our knowledge from 5 or 10 years ago. We must continuously research new trends, methodologies, music, and techniques. The best teachers actively research current trends, by following the news, reading books, listening to new music, attending conferences, and finding fun and interesting ways to increase their knowledge and improve their skills in their teaching areas. To be a strong role model to students, teachers should be engaged in continuous learning and ongoing career development. Stay curious.

Getting an Education

Earning a degree is not always a hard and fast requirement for teaching. If you are teaching privately it could be helpful to have a music college or conservatory degree, in order to attract students. Some good private teachers don't have degrees. They usually have other credentials, such as performing locally on a regular basis or being featured on high-profile gigs and recordings. Most schools will require a minimum of a bachelor's degree to apply for a job teaching music. Many colleges ask for at least a master's degree.

High schools, elementary schools, and middle schools usually look for a degree in music education, although they might hire a music teacher who can also teach outside subjects, depending on the size and the type of the school. Many public schools require state certification, which must accompany a degree in music education. In order to receive their degree and be certified, student teachers must complete a teaching practicum, which involves observing and being observed in the classroom.

Colleges hiring music professors will often look for more specialized degrees related to the area of teaching and courses to be taught. This makes sense, since if you are in college to study composition, for example, you would likely want a teacher who was a composer and who had studied composition themselves. It takes a trained guitarist to teach college-level guitar students, to give another example. For college teaching, a music education degree is good mostly for teaching music education courses.

Some teachers teach across musical disciplines. They may have degrees in performance, but be able to also teach music business, songwriting, or arranging and production. For this kind of teaching, you will need a portfolio of your work, to show your skills in the areas you intend to teach. Sometimes flexibility and the ability to teach across disciplines can be a big plus for schools looking to hire one person to cover a variety of courses. Other times, a college may be looking for a specialty, such as marching band, composition, chorus, jazz, or a specific instrument like harp or trombone.

Getting a college degree is a good opportunity to build a variety of skills, whether in production, business, writing, performing, or any other area related or unrelated to your major or minor. Those wishing to teach in college should plan on pursuing a master's degree. If you are shopping for a music degree, one good resource is the *Barron's Profiles of American Colleges* which is published every year. You could also talk to a high school guidance counselor, or visit a local educational resource center, a library, teachers, professional musicians, and of course Google is always a terrific tool for searching for more info on schools and degree programs. You could also engage with a specialized music college admissions consultant.

Career Planning

Think ahead and try to imagine what your career might look like in the short, mid, and long term. Some musicians focus on their artist careers first, and then develop teaching careers afterwards. Others are focused on becoming teachers right away.

Use the personal and professional self-assessment in Chapter 2. Write down what you want your career to look like in 5, 10, and 20 years. Writing things down on paper is a way to make your plans more tangible and real. You can also show your plan to counselors and others who may have important suggestions or information for you to consider in light of your specific goals.

In my own case, I started out teaching privately while I was earning my college music degree. During those years, I was employed by a small neighborhood music store near my home in Medford, MA. That led to other opportunities, such as teaching at other stores and managing the store's school instrument rental program. This was an excellent opportunity to learn on the job, and I developed organized teaching methods and approaches for different types of students at all levels and ages. It also provided a steady stream of income I could use to pay my rent and other bills during and after college. The money I earned from teaching helped me repay my student loans.

A few years later, I was asked to teach classes part-time at Berklee College of Music in Boston, where I had earned my bachelor's degree. This was my first taste of classroom teaching. I remember being nervous about it just before I started. One of my mentors, Rob Rose, shared a really important piece of advice (paraphrasing): "There are two things you need to be a good teacher. You have to know your subject, and enjoy sharing that knowledge with others." Later, I received many valuable tips from my department heads and deans. Much of the advice was fairly common sense, such as to learn all my students' names. As I gained more experience, I became more confident as a teacher.

You can't know exactly where your career path will lead. Forming a set of clear (written) goals, considering the obstacles that exist, how to overcome those obstacles, and learning to recognize opportunities are how you begin. Revisit your goals regularly. These are the career planning techniques I keep returning to.

Classroom Teaching Versus Private Studio

As I described, my own experience includes teaching privately and also classroom teaching of various music subjects. I have presented master classes and workshops on music and music education all over the globe. I've shared enthusiastically in the successes of many of my former students. There are some important but interesting differences to consider when it comes to the kinds of teaching you may find yourself doing. Facing a large lecture hall full of hundreds of students is a vastly different challenge compared to teaching a single student sitting in front of you.

I liken teaching in front of a group to a musical performance. It's important to get the audience's attention early and maintain it throughout.

Keeping your presentation short and concise, speaking loudly and clearly, making eye contact with members of the audience, appropriate pacing, and having a strong conclusion are all important aspects to pay attention to.

As with public speaking, understanding certain techniques will help you do well. Channeling any nervousness into a productive outcome is one such technique. *Stage fright* is not limited to just performing! Judicious use of humor can be an effective tool. I made it my habit to observe public speakers and master teachers and to take note of any techniques they use. (I also observed less-experienced speakers to learn what NOT to do.) I found certain TED Talks on public speaking to be helpful, such as Harvard professor Amy Cuddy's presentation on the research into *body language* and *power poses*.

At the opposite end of the spectrum, with a private studio student you have a chance to really get to know them. You can quickly ascertain their level of musical knowledge and ability, assess how they learn, and map out a strategy for their progress. It's rewarding to see growth in your individual students over time, and understand your own role in that progress. You get to learn their strengths and weaknesses and find new ways to help them learn. The teacher–student relationship becomes highly personalized in this setting.

It's vital that you inspire them to learn. One way to do this is to display your own mastery without showing off. If you can demonstrate your own skill in a way that makes them feel they can learn from you and show them the steps they can take to progress, your most eager students will be grateful to you and remember their lesson times fondly. One of the most rewarding things about teaching is when your students come back years later (sometimes many years) to tell you what a positive impact you had on them and their learning.

Whether in the classroom or studio, a teacher can't know everything. It's fine to admit when you don't know the answer to a student's question or when you were wrong in the past. Honesty and transparency engender respect and admiration from students, and students can easily sense if you are trying to fool them. When you are able, it's important to answer students' questions in a clear way that everyone can understand. You know you are doing it right when you see the light bulb switch on above their head.

Show the Way

Remember that for every accomplished person, they once didn't know all that much. We all had to learn and, at the beginning, we needed teachers to show us the way. Teaching music is something you are called to do as a vocation. While there is money to be earned, one shouldn't do it just for the money (there are certainly easier ways to earn money). You could be a part-time or full-time teacher, and combine that role with just about any other kind of career.

I clearly remember a metaphor shared often with me by my father, who was a professor at Cornell University. He said he felt like a mother bird in the nest, going around to each student to deposit a small bit of knowledge in their eager minds, just as the mother bird would deposit a morsel of food in each of her chicks' wide open beaks. As a teacher now myself, this image resonates strongly with me. If you think teaching is in your future, seek out other teachers you admire and respect and ask them to share their secrets with you. Teaching is one of the best ways to keep learning, and if you love music, you might love teaching it to others as well.

Action Step:
Consider if you want to teach, and if so, what kind of teaching would be most appealing and enjoyable for you. Will teaching be your main job, or will you do it as a side job?

How to Scale a Teaching Business

Scaling a business means growing profits exponentially. The term *scale* is used in entrepreneurial circles to refer to the potential for a business to grow from startup phase, to serving large numbers of customers. Software is the ultimate scalable business, since once a software program has been created, you can add customers without using more money to create each copy. To attract new customers, you might need to put some money into marketing, but you won't need to build the program again every time someone makes a purchase. It costs nothing extra to scale up users in terms of providing the product. Is it possible to scale a teaching business? It turns out the answer is yes.

Let's zoom out for a moment. Like a lawyer, a teacher is usually paid by the hour. Even if the hourly rate is very high, the lawyer and the teacher are limited by the number of hours they can work. Is it realistic to work 40 hours a week? 80 hours? This means that there's always going to be a limit on earnings, because the number of hours that a human can work has an upper limit. There's nothing wrong with working and being paid by the hour, but it doesn't allow for scaling a teaching business very far.

So how could scale be accomplished? Let's look at an example.

Let's say that every week you will film a short instructional video, and post it on your website. You can do this 52 weeks in a year. You set up your site with the videos behind a paywall. Students can pay you $1.00 each week to access the video, or subscribe for a monthly, semi-annual, or annual fee to view them all. Once a student has paid the fee, they have access to the videos indefinitely. Next, you do some clever marketing on social media, using SEO and SEM techniques. This might be free or it might cost you a few bucks, depending on your strategy. You can offer free access for a limited time and other promotions.

Over time, you attract several hundred subscribers, then several thousand. At a certain point, you have 100,000 subscribers, paying you a dollar a week, more or less. That's something like $300,000.00 a MONTH—and a multimillion dollar annual income. I once read about a guitar teacher in the United Kingdom who did exactly this. I can think of other ways to scale a teaching business, but this example should give you some food for thought, at least. As an entrepreneur, you should always think about how you will scale your business.

Action Step:
Consider the ways you could scale your business, teaching or otherwise. What kind of income would you like to earn from your business? Don't be afraid to aim high!

CHAPTER 15

Entrepreneurship and Psychology: How to Improve Your Thinking to Enhance Success

There is nothing either good or bad, but thinking makes it so.
—William Shakespeare, Hamlet, Act [2], Scene [2]

Mental Attitudes Matter

There's no shortage of outstanding books, blogs, and articles that examine the *entrepreneurial mindset*. Books such as *How to Win Friends and Influence People* by Dale Carnegie, first published in 1936, sold more than 15 million copies, making it one of the best-selling books of all time. Other books dive deep into the psyche of the successful artist or business leader, closely examining the link between thinking and success.

Emergent artists, nascent entrepreneurs, and business owners should put aside some time each day just to think deeply about what's going on. "Aha moments" can occur anytime, and cultivating organized and disciplined thought patterns will increase the frequency and quality of your revelations. Carefully consider how thinking affects the actions of our partners, clients, superiors, collaborators, and fans. Cultivating awareness of your own thinking, and its connection to and influence on outcomes, is a lifelong endeavor. You'll discover countless immediately useful and actionable ideas from reading, and taking time to think.

Studying the seminal thinkers from fields outside of music, such as psychology, economics, statistics, philosophy, and especially business, can lead to breakthroughs in thinking, which enhance career advancement, artistic and professional development, improved professional relationships, and effective networking.

Metacognition and Meta-Skills

Thinking about thinking is called *metacognition*. Analyzing your own and others' thinking will help you to recognize and create opportunities, spot the obstacles to success, and develop the right strategies to reach your goals. Thinking deeply about what you want out of your music career and your life will almost certainly play a big role in your success, or lack of it. Of course, luck also plays a role, as it does in everything. How you think about your luck can sometimes create more of it, whether good or bad. Metacognition is the ability to examine your own thinking dispassionately and understand how it affects your career and life outcomes.

Meta-skills refers to higher-order functional expertise that can be applied in different areas, such as self-awareness, critical thinking, interviewing, storytelling, empathy, and learning. These skills help us to be more effective in all we do, are permanent, and allow us to build other transitory skills.

Action Step:
Make a list of meta-skills you either already possess or would like to acquire.

Your Thinking Will Change

Over time, as you grow and learn, and the business environment changes, your thinking will also be transformed. In the introduction to this book, I wrote about how my own thinking had changed, from someone who eschewed and abhorred the business aspects of a music career to one who came to fully embrace it. While there were many epiphanies along the way, the transformation in my thinking was not inevitable. I kept an open mind, considered where I might have previously been wrong in my thinking, and changed my mind with my new knowledge and perspectives.

While no one can see the future, you can think about your future career in any number of ways. For example, consider where the things you do exceptionally well intersect with an established need in the market-place. If you're good at something, but there is no need for it, that doesn't mean you should stop doing it. Instead, you might do it solely for your own satisfaction, and earn your living doing something else.

Imagine you are a fiddle player, and at the moment there is little interest in or demand for fiddle players. Most fiddle players will give up trying to make a living playing the fiddle. After a while, there could be a resurgence in demand, or the fact that there are so few professional fiddle players left will mean that those that remain will be in high demand.

Conditions change and so will you. As you grow into your career, you figure out what your strengths are, and where your talents and skills are most needed. You leverage your opportunities and learn to overcome obstacles. You improve your skills and gain valuable experience, which helps you accomplish even more. You come to love doing those things you are good at, because it sustains your living.

Later in your career, you might reassess all you believe to be true and perhaps adjust your goals in light of your achievements. Later on, you might choose to focus on only one or two aspects of your career, as you realize you have less time left to reach all of your goals. This doesn't mean you give up on your dreams, but you take a realistic approach based on what can reasonably be expected. We can't know what will happen, but we do know that the future will look different.

Metacognition is an important and useful tool for analyzing and understanding yourself and your relationship to the world.

Action Steps:
Pay attention to your thinking, be aware of any changes, and seek out inspirational sources to help you develop your thought-based techniques. Be especially wary of thought patterns or emotions that can hold you back, such as excessive negativity, anger, and resistance to change. Observe how your thinking affects how you feel about your career and the world. Consider that every great achievement in the history of humankind started with thinking. Cultivate self-awareness. Harness your thinking as the incredibly powerful tool that it is.

Brainstorming Opportunities

Brainstorming is the practice of thinking about every possibility and idea, usually together with other smart and accomplished people. The goal of brainstorming is to envision all possibilities and identify all possible paths forward, with the understanding that many, or most, are not the correct ones. It takes fertilizer to make the grass grow. Songwriters know they have to write many bad songs to get a few good ones. This is the nature of brainstorming.

As a professor and advisor, I brainstorm with my high-achieving students every day. Sometimes they are paralyzed because they see too many opportunities. Other times, they might struggle to see any way forward. Thinking together with someone else about logical next steps is a useful exercise. It helps to field various ideas with the understanding that not all will be appropriate or actionable. One useful approach I've suggested is to analyze others who came before, and examine their strategies and actions to try to understand their thinking in light of the outcomes. This is where the rubber meets the road. A music careerist will continually (re)establish goals, using self-awareness, their own experience, plus the experience of others to chart a way forward. As Napoleon Hill said: "Goals are dreams with a deadline."

Recognizing Obstacles, Cultivating Ability

Thinking deeply about your goals is not enough. Write your specific goals down and share them with other more experienced, believable people to get their feedback. Some might tell you your goals are difficult or even impossible to achieve. Don't be offended. They are just sharing their perspective. You might know more than they do, after all, and they could be wrong. Consider their points carefully and try to understand their argument. They might have helped you by pointing out a previously unforeseen obstacle for you to take into consideration.

Any goal worth striving for will have obstacles. For musicians, the single biggest obstacle is often competition. The demand isn't great enough to support all the talented musicians and to provide them with viable careers. The concepts in this book should help you differentiate yourself and your music from your competitors and give you a greater chance for success. Positioning yourself against your direct competitors is a way to overcome the obstacle of competition and gain fans, as we learned when researching and writing the marketing section of the business plan in Chapter 5.

Other obstacles to success can be external or internal (i.e., your thinking). While pure luck usually plays some part, you can do several things to leverage the opportunities in front of you. First, take the time to learn about your obstacles. If you've set your goals properly, written them down, and shared them with others, you should have an idea of what the obstacles are. Don't fear them, as you must eventually face them squarely to overcome. Write down your obstacles next to the goals, and categorize them in a way that makes sense to you. Then, prioritize in order of importance and difficulty.

There might be some things you can work on immediately, and others may take more time. Use the SMART goals framework to describe your response to each obstacle. Remember, your plans should be:

- Specific
- Measurable
- Attainable
- Relevant
- Time-based

(See also Figure 2.2.)

I like to say that the biggest room around is the room for improvement. No matter what level you are at, you can identify specific areas of your knowledge and skills that could be improved. You should be motivated to work on improving even your strongest areas, because it will cause those pesky obstacles to melt away. If you have areas of real weakness, you might consider having someone else help you with those. Play to your strengths.

Continually assessing your goals, identifying obstacles, and strategizing how to overcome them is a framework for enduring success in business. If you train yourself to think this way, you'll grow more skilled and capable in managing the business aspects of your music business and art.

In this final chapter of the book, I will now return to the topic of leadership in business and music management.

Executive Leadership and Time Management

Building a business in music offers plenty of opportunities to learn *leadership skills*. Being an orchestra conductor is a lot like being the CEO of a company. Juggling resources and egos, casting the vision, crafting a mission statement, teambuilding, focusing on innovation while fostering creativity in others, managing operations, securing budgets, attracting clients, overseeing branding and marketing—you'll have a seemingly endless to-do list. With so much going on, *time management* is perhaps the most important leadership skill. Time imposes limits on us all, so learning to effectively manage your time is an important meta-skill.

I recognized that working in music offers ways to learn how to effectively lead. As I became a student of executive leadership, I attended conferences, read widely, observed and consulted with other leaders, and then experimented with my new knowledge tools. As a bandleader, I used my newfound techniques to guide performing groups. Learning about leadership became a passion, and I'm grateful for each and every opportunity I've had to lead. I've made plenty of mistakes and taken the learning from those lumps.

You must learn how to become a leader while on the job. As you progress, you will have the chance to observe how others do it and build understanding of what works best, and also what doesn't work as well. Every team has a unique dynamic, and not all techniques will work with every team. Be alert to the learning you can glean from each situation. Explore your own philosophies about how to lead, and work to become a better leader.

Leadership Philosophy

Everyone develops their own ideas of what works when it comes to leadership and how best to achieve shared objectives. We learn by trial and error. Motivating people to work in tandem to achieve complex goals is not easy. Our failures teach us what doesn't work. We should also learn from the failures of others. Books on leadership philosophy and *organizational behavior* abound, and advanced leadership training is offered at major universities and by companies.

Businesses need leadership to succeed. Most organizations have in place a *management structure* with a hierarchy, to set goals, devise strategy, and guide execution. In theory, the higher one is in the hierarchy, the more responsibility they have for decision making. At the bottom, workers perform the work, usually by serving customers, making products, or delivering services. In order to be effective, information must flow up and down the management chain. As anyone who has ever worked in a large organization will tell you, this doesn't always happen. Sometimes *silos* develop, where information is hoarded and not shared, for one reason or another.

Over a long time, I've developed some opinions on management styles, and in particular the ones with which I'm most and least comfortable. I prefer the *bottom-up* approach as opposed to the *top-down* management style. I'll explain what this means, and why I prefer bottom-up to top-down management.

Top Down Versus Bottom Up

These quotes I've shared earlier sum up my feelings about leadership in business:

Steve Jobs said, "It doesn't make sense to hire smart people and tell them what to do; we hire smart people so they can tell us what to do."

Richard Branson says, "Clients do not come first. Employees come first. If you take care of your employees, they will take care of the clients."

The person at the top sets the tone for the entire organization. We are hard-wired by evolution to follow leaders, for our very survival. There's an ancient Chinese proverb which says "The fish rots from the head," meaning that when an organization is struggling it is always the fault of the leader. Management gets the credit when things go well, and they deserve the blame when things are going wrong. After all, they are the ones making the decisions. The very few times in my life I've had to fire someone, I took the responsibility for it. It was my mistake to hire that person in the first place.

Choreographer Otis Sallid once told me: "Never commit to someone who won't commit to your commitment." It took me a moment to understand his point. For example, as a bandleader I make a commitment to my client to start on time. If a musician is late arriving at the bandstand, they have jeopardized my ability to fulfill my commitment to my client. That could happen once to anyone. If it becomes habitual, there's a problem.

Employees behave in a way that is dictated by the chain of command. Or do they?

It's the leader's job to articulate and communicate the vision and mission. The people tasked with doing the actual work should have a say in how the work is to be done. After all, they were hired presumably because they know what needs to be done and how to do it. Completing the work is the *strategic imperative*. When employees have a say in the design of their work, they will be more committed. We call this *buy-in*. They teach this stuff in business schools.

I believe that the dictatorial style—my way or the highway—doesn't work as well. Stanford professor, best-selling author, and management consultant James C. Collins says you have to "get the right people on the bus." The leader can't do everything, that's why they need employees. The leader's problem isn't usually a skills or training issue, it's a *selection* problem. Get the best people you can, and have them tell you how the work should be accomplished.

Leader as Servant

Internet entrepreneur and CEO Tony Hsieh puts it this way: "The best leaders are servant leaders—they serve those they lead." You can find a lot of literature on the topic of *servant leadership, conscious capitalism*, and *values-led business*, which seems to indicate that taking care of the people under you is smart business practice. Billionaire Hamdi Ulukaya, founder of Chobani Yogurt, has given a TED Talk on this subject, which he titled "The Anti-CEO Playbook." Hamdi emphasizes *stakeholder capitalism* over shareholder capitalism and challenges leaders to care deeply about the people working under them and the communities they serve.

It's not a new idea that companies shouldn't exist only for the benefit of their owners and customers. Henry Ford realized that in order for his Model T automobile to be a commercial success, the workers on his assembly lines had to be paid well enough to afford one.

This concept applies equally to the music industry. After all, who wants to watch unhappy musicians on stage? As a bandleader, I've developed strategies to keep my musicians happy. I want them to enjoy playing in my band. It's not always easy, since we face challenges with every gig. I pay them fairly, and I make sure that their working conditions are tolerable. I keep open lines of communication and encourage a culture where everyone is accepted and valued for who they are and what they do. It's really not that complicated: I treat others the same way I'd like to be treated.

The Role of Failure

I wrote this book to help you succeed in the music industry. We cannot talk about success without discussing the importance of failure. If you look at any successful entrepreneur, you will invariably find they have had business failures in the past. Even Steve Jobs of Apple was fired from his own company. When he returned, they reached new heights together. Failure is a crucial ingredient for success, as odd as that might sound. Understanding the role failure plays in success, and more importantly, how you react to failure, is extremely important.

I've seen the term "fail up." While I'm not exactly certain what this means, it suggests to me that we should always strive to learn from failure. We should use our failures to better ourselves. At the very least, we should learn from our failures so that we don't make the same mistakes again. Failure is the universe teaching us what not to do.

Failure is simply the opportunity to begin again, this time more intelligently.

—Henry Ford

I've seen this acronym: F.E.A.R. = False Evidence Appearing Real

It's normal to be afraid of failure. But, you shouldn't be. Knowing what won't work is a component of knowing what will likely work best. As a leader in the music industry, learn to embrace failure. You will get rejected at auditions. You might not get into the school you want to go to. You might be passed over for the job you really want. Your prospective client may hire someone else. Your fans might forget about you. All of this is normal and accompanies the risk of being in business. There are no guarantees you will succeed at all. But that should never stop you from doing your very best under the circumstances.

Postscript

Taking Care of Yourself:
How to Prevent Hearing Loss
from Loud Music

Many musicians struggle with *hearing loss* as they age, and it can be easily prevented by using special musicians' earplugs. Every young musician should get their hearing tested by an *audiologist*, and use these earplugs religiously. Tinnitus and other hearing problems can be very serious. Hearing loss experienced by musicians is a serious occupational hazard. You should also know what to do if you experience a sudden catastrophic event with your hearing.

Musicians commonly suffer from hearing loss over time. Most older musicians report some level of decline, and more than a few accomplished musicians become completely deaf by the time they reach middle age. Beethoven is but one famous example. Though he continued to compose music, he suffered from depression in his later years at least partly due to having lost the ability to hear his own compositions. Many older rock musicians have also lost most or all of their hearing (this author included). Some have been forced to give up performing live. The really sad thing about this is that it can be so easily prevented.

During a recent ensemble performance class I teach at Berklee College of Music, students were playing arrangements of current and older pop, funk, rock, and jazz popular hits. After the two-hour rehearsal, I asked them how many were wearing hearing protection. Not one student raised their hand. I wasn't shocked, because when I was a student I never wore earplugs either. I now regret it and wish I could go back and do this period of my life over. I have lost 80 percent of my hearing in my left ear and 30 percent in my right ear. While I can hear very little with my left ear, my right ear is still fairly functional, so it's not all gloom and doom.

The doctor told me I need to take measures if I want to preserve the hearing I have left. I now religiously wear specially fitted musicians' earplugs. I showed them to my students. I'll tell you more about these earplugs next, but I told my class that any student that would get their hearing tested and get a pair of those special earplugs would get an automatic "A" grade for the course.

If you are a musician, what could be more important than your hearing? Don't be foolish (as I was). Protect your hearing so you will still have it in your later years. It's possible to lose your hearing completely, whether it happens in one moment or over a long period of time. Besides testing and getting the right kind of protection, you should also know what to do in the case of a catastrophic event with your hearing. This last item I wish I had known earlier, because that is how I lost the hearing in my left ear. As you learn about how to protect your hearing, you should also learn about how the ear functions and which kinds of situations pose the most danger.

What Is Hearing Loss and What Causes It?

The ear is a delicate piece of machinery. While this is not meant to be a medical synopsis, you should know that our ears have three main areas: the outer ear, the middle ear, and the inner ear (Figure P.1). The outer ear is the part you can see. The middle ear starts with the eardrum, also called the *tympanic membrane*, and includes three tiny bones linked together called the *ossicular chain* that transmits the sound from the eardrum to the *oval window* of the inner ear. The bones in the ossicular chain, called *ossicles*, are among the smallest in the human body. The inner ear includes the *cochlea*, which is a fluid-filled spiral tube with tiny hair cells known as *cilia* that connect to the *auditory nerve* which transmits impulses to the centers of the brain responsible for hearing. The inner ear also contains the *vestibular system* which is responsible for sensing motion and balance.

Hearing loss occurs when there is damage to any of these components. If the ossicles are damaged there would be a lack of transmission of sound to the inner ear from the eardrum. If the eardrum is punctured or torn it will not function properly in sensing sound vibrations from the air. If the hair cells are damaged, the sound will not be transmitted to the

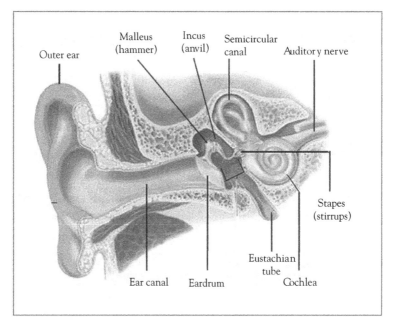

Figure P.1 The ear

auditory nerve. There can even be damage to the nerve itself, or a tumor in the brain causing hearing loss.

As humans, our hearing apparatus is incredibly sensitive and complicated and there are even some mysteries we don't have explanations for. For example, little is known about what happens in the brain and how we identify the various frequencies of sound waves after they've been processed by the ear and the auditory nerve. Healthy hearing can be disrupted in many ways, from physical damage to disease. If you are serious about your music, you should be serious about protecting your hearing. Let's take a closer look at how to do so.

How You Can Protect Your Hearing

One of the most common causes of hearing loss is loud sounds. The louder the sound, the more damage it can cause to your hearing. We measure both sound intensity and the perceived loudness of sounds using the *decibel scale*. A doubling of perceived loudness is represented by an increase of 10 decibels, although the actual sound energy increase represented is much greater than that. It's important to understand that the decibel scale is a logarithmic scale, not a linear scale. According to acousticians and doctors, any sound above 85 decibels can damage your hearing. Musical instruments, and especially amplified music, or drumming, can easily reach levels much higher than this.

Other factors can contribute to the danger of damage from loud sounds. Your distance from the sound source matters, as does the duration of the sound. A very loud sound of short duration, such as a single gunshot, may not pose as much of a hazard as exposure to prolonged sound pressure, such as at a rock concert. Therefore, musicians (and everyone, actually) should always wear some kind of ear protection when around loud sounds, whether performing, rehearsing, at a concert or club, or in any environment where there could be danger (such as a workplace), whether intermittent or prolonged in duration.

It's easy to say "use hearing protection" but in reality there are many kinds of earplugs or hearing protection devices, and not all are created equal. I'll give you a rundown on what is available and what you should use, but first let's talk about where to go to get your hearing tested. You will need to have your hearing tested in order to get the right kind of protection.

Testing by an Audiologist

I strongly recommend visiting an audiology laboratory to get your hearing tested. You can find an audiologist to test you at any major hospital center or large university. I've been going to the Audiology Laboratory at Northeastern University in Boston for many years, and the testing is free. It usually takes about an hour. They put you in this little room that is superinsulated for sound, and the technician sits on the other side of a double-paned window. You put on a pair of comfy audiophile headphones and they play you little beeps and tones in a variety of frequency ranges, slowly decreasing the volume. Every time you hear a tone, you signal to them with your hand or by pressing a button. Then they start mixing in some background noise while they play other sounds or words and ask you to signal when you hear something. At the end they will give you a printout showing your hearing response in all audible frequency ranges.

It's very interesting to see where you might hear one frequency better than others, and you will learn the highest and lowest frequencies you can hear. More importantly, if you do this regularly, you can keep an eye on your hearing and find out over time if there is any degradation in your ability to hear. I recommend getting tested every two to three years.

Action Step:
Get your hearing tested by an audiologist.

Types of Hearing Protection

After your test, the audiologist can order you a pair of specially made musicians' earplugs. This is the best part. They inject foam into your ears which hardens after just a few minutes. Then they send the mold of your ear out to a special lab that makes silicone earplugs that fit exactly to the shape of your ears. They are labeled so you know one is for the left and one is for the right. Fitted to the silicone ear-mold is a tiny attenuator which can be removed. (*Note*: An *attenuator* is a small filter which lowers the decibel level with flat response across all frequencies.) The attenuator is usually –15 or –20 decibels, which means the sound pressure will be reduced evenly so you can hear everything exactly the same, but at a lower, safer volume. What I like about the musicians' earplugs system is that you can increase the attenuation by swapping out the little filters. So, for softer music where I still want protection I use the 15 decibel attenuators, and I use the 20 or 25 decibel ones for louder music.

These are the best earplugs available and they are also super comfortable, unlike the store-bought ones that are one-size-fits-all. The foam or soft silicone putty earplugs they sell at the pharmacy work well, are inexpensive, and certainly better than nothing, but they always become uncomfortable if you leave them in for very long. With the musicians' earplugs (that's what they're called) you can leave them in for extended periods of time, and you will forget you are wearing them because they fit so comfortably in your ear canal.

Dangerous Conditions to Watch Out for

Have you ever been out at a concert or a loud dance club for an evening, and noticed a ringing or high-pitched tone in your ears afterwards? You may have sustained hearing damage. While the ear will often recover from this in a day or so, if you repeat the experience too often you may end up with a condition called *tinnitus* (pronounced: TIN-ni-tus). This annoying condition can be best described as a constant ringing or high-pitched tone that never goes away. People who suffer from tinnitus typically experience variation in the intensity and loudness of the tone; it can be maddeningly loud at times and then barely noticeable, but it's always present.

Tinnitus can interfere with proper hearing and also diminish the overall quality of life. Many musicians suffer from the condition as a result of years of unprotected exposure to loud sounds, and it is one of the most common forms of hearing degradation. While many people hear ringing in their ears from time to time, tinnitus is a serious condition and there is no treatment for it as of yet. The rule of thumb should be that whenever you know you might be exposed to loud sounds, you should carry your earplugs with you and put them in at the first sign of danger. I try to keep a pair on me at all times, literally. It's better to have them and not need them, than to need them and not have them!

Besides concerts and clubs, the cinema, sporting events, or political rallies, anywhere sound reinforcement (public address systems) or music amplification equipment is in use can pose a danger. Even noisy street traffic can be dangerous if you are exposed to it for long periods. I wear noise-cancelling headphones in the subway, where besides the screeching of wheels, public announcements can be excruciatingly loud. Acoustic musical instruments are generally less hazardous, but if you were in an enclosed rehearsal space with a symphony orchestra, that would undoubtedly call for hearing protection.

Headphone use can be dangerous, too. Never turn up music loud when wearing headphones, and if you are listening for long periods using headphones, be sure to take regular breaks to rest your ears. Remember that it's not only sound pressure, but duration of the sound that adds to the danger. Factory workers and machine operators are usually required to wear hearing protection, and high- and low-frequency sounds outside of our audible range can cause damage when at high amplitude. This means your hearing could be damaged by sounds you can't even hear. The Occupational Safety and Health Administration (known as OSHA) is a federal agency that tests for these kinds of frequencies when monitoring workplace safety conditions.

What to Do If You Have Sudden Hearing Loss

If you experience an event which you feel may have caused trauma to your ears, whether from loud sounds or a foreign item in your ear, the first thing to do is visit an emergency room immediately. If your city has a specialty hospital or clinic for ear health (in Boston we have Mass Eye and Ear Hospital), go there as quickly as possible and tell the doctor what happened. If you have sustained damage to your ears there are measures you can take which could be important to saving your future hearing, but they must be undertaken quickly. For example, steroids can be used to reduce swelling, which might limit damage to the sensitive parts of your middle or inner ear. Always refer to a doctor about any potential ear damage, preferably a specialist, and do it quickly.

Use of In-Ear Monitors and Headphones

In-ear monitors can be used to limit sound pressure in a noisy stage environment, but I'm not certain they provide the same level of protection as do the musicians' earplugs. If you can control the volume, and they seal off your ear canal tightly, they should provide some protection. The point is not to turn them up too loud or keep them in for extended periods.

The same applies to headphone use. Be very careful to read the manufacturer's instructions as they will often contain information about the dangers of hearing loss while using the headphones. It's been documented that using headphones turned up loud or for long periods can cause hearing damage and hearing loss. This also applies to the ear buds people use with their smartphones.

Playing It Safe

You only get one set of ears, so you'd better take good care of them, especially if you are a musician. You depend on them for your profession and your pleasure so you want them to last a lifetime. As the old expression goes: Better safe than sorry. Get tested, get earplugs, carry them with you, and use them whenever there is any chance of danger from loud sounds or loud music. It can take a little getting used to, but once you acclimate to them you won't even know you are wearing them. It's definitely possible to have effective hearing protection that is comfortable and natural sounding. In my experience, the most difficult thing is to remember to carry them with me. I had to make an effort to make it a habit. Even though I've lost a portion of my valuable hearing ability, which is frustrating, I am determined to protect what I have left. I'm going to need it.

About the Author

Tom Stein is an international musician, leading music educator, global music industry and educational consultant, and a cultural diplomat. Tom has been professionally active in the music industry for over 40 years and has performed in over 30 countries on guitar, electric bass, and voice. As a senior professor at Berklee College of Music in Boston, Tom has taught thousands of students, many who have gone on to illustrious music careers, winning GRAMMY awards, recording hit records, and touring the globe to give concerts. He is a member of the Fulbright Specialist Roster with the U.S. State Department.

Tom earned his Bachelor of Music in guitar performance, arranging, and music business with top honors at Berklee College of Music, and his Master of Music in Jazz Studies, Performance on electric bass from New England Conservatory. He has been on faculty at Berklee since 1988 where he's taught courses in music theory, improvisation, ear-training (solfege), arranging, music production, music education, and music business. Tom produces concerts and also performs live and in the studio on bass, guitar, and voice. He also plays Appalachian mountain dulcimer and is a proficient arranger and producer of high-profile events. In 2014 he produced and presented a concert series representing the music of the United States in Shanghai, China, at the Shanghai Concert Hall in People's Park.

His concert reel is here: https://youtube.com/watch?v=_XBTe58VoP0

Index

OTHER TITLES IN THE SPORTS AND ENTERTAINMENT MANAGEMENT AND MARKETING COLLECTION

Lynn Kahle, University of Oregon, Editor

- *The Business of Music Management* by Tom Stein
- *The Olympic Sports Economy* by Max Donner
- *Great Coaching and Your Bottom Line* by Marijan Hizak
- *Artist Development Essentials* by Hristo Penchev

Concise and Applied Business Books

The Collection listed above is one of 30 business subject collections that Business Expert Press has grown to make BEP a premiere publisher of print and digital books. Our concise and applied books are for...

- Professionals and Practitioners
- Faculty who adopt our books for courses
- Librarians who know that BEP's Digital Libraries are a unique way to offer students ebooks to download, not restricted with any digital rights management
- Executive Training Course Leaders
- Business Seminar Organizers

Business Expert Press books are for anyone who needs to dig deeper on business ideas, goals, and solutions to everyday problems. Whether one print book, one ebook, or buying a digital library of 110 ebooks, we remain the affordable and smart way to be business smart. For more information, please visit www.businessexpertpress.com, or contact sales@businessexpertpress.com.

CPSIA information can be obtained
at www.ICGtesting.com
Printed in the USA
BVHW091938120921
616573BV00003B/9